Historic
Battleship *Texas*
The Last Dreadnought

John C. Ferguson

Historic
Battleship *Texas*
The Last Dreadnought

John C. Ferguson

StateHouse
Press
McMurry University
Abilene, Texas

Library of Congress Cataloging-in-Publication Data

Ferguson, John C.
Historic Battleship Texas: the last dreadnought / John C. Ferguson.
   p. cm. — (Military history of texas series; No. 4)
Includes bibliographical references and index.
ISBN-13: 978-1-933337-07-4 (pbk.: alk. paper)
ISBN-10: 1-933337-07-9 (pbk.: alk. paper)
1. Texas (Battleship) I. Title.

VA65.T44F47 2007
359.8'352--dc22

                                                2007028523

State House Press
McMurry Station, Box 637
Abilene, TX 79697-0637
(325) 572-3974
www.mcwhiney.org/press

ISBN-10: 1-933337-07-9
ISBN-13: 978-1-933337-07-4

10 9 8 7 6 5 4 3 2 1

Distributed by Texas A&M University Press Consortium
1-800-826-8911 • www.tamu.edu/upress

Book designed by Rosenbohm Graphic Design

Dedication

To George and the boys; the hard-working, underpaid, and often unappreciated men who work to maintain and preserve her every day. And to Ed Morrison, who loved the *Texas*.

MILITARY HISTORY OF TEXAS SERIES: NUMBER FOUR

The Military History of Texas Series tells the colorful, dynamic, and heroic stories of the state's soldiers, battles, and battlefields from Spanish times to the present. The series promotes State House Press's mission to encourage traditional narratives and make history accessible to the broadest audience possible.

ALSO IN THE MILITARY HISTORY OF TEXAS SERIES

The Finishing Stroke: Texans in the 1864 Tennessee Campaign
    by John R. Lundberg

The Wings of Change: The Army Air Force Experience in Texas During World War II
    by Thomas E. Alexander

Sacrificed at the Alamo: Tradegy and Triumph in the Texas Revolution
    by Richard Bruce Winders

Table of Contents

List of Photographs

Photos on cover and page 168 courtesy of C. Tom Scott. All other photos courtesy of Battleship *Texas* State Historic Site.

List of Maps

All maps by Robert F. Pace.

INTRODUCTION

The landing craft circled incessantly.

Shortly after midnight, the infantry soldiers who had been able to drift off to sleep awoke as the galleys on the Navy ships served up the traditional pre-invasion breakfast of steak and eggs to these nervous but determined young soldiers. In the pre-dawn darkness after the men had eaten, the various ship captains on the many troop transports gave the order, "Land the landing force!" In each of the troop carriers, the heavily laden soldiers of the assault battalions made their way up to the main decks. Once there, they clambered over the sides of the ships and crawled down the swaying rope cargo nets into the small Higgins boats bobbing on the surface of the sea far below.[1]

Once in the landing craft the soldiers' torment intensified. As each Higgins boat filled with a platoon of thirty-six men, the coxswain (or driver) of the boat pulled it away from the troop transport and another landing craft took its place to take on more precious human cargo. The Higgins boats and other landing craft already filled with troops circled the mother ships, waiting until all of the soldiers making up the initial assault wave were on board. As the boats circled, they pitched and rolled in the rough, storm-tossed English Channel. The motion of the boats, combined with the diesel fumes from their engines, made some soldiers ill. Many of them lost their carefully prepared breakfasts, causing other soldiers to become nauseated as well. After more than an hour of the continuous circling in the vomit-lined landing craft, drenched to the skin from the ocean spray, chilled to the bone, most of the soldiers would attack anything, face any enemy, just to get out of the boats.

Finally, after what seemed an eternity, it was time to begin the attack. The boats moved away from the transport ships and formed into a line, with dozens of the small Higgins boats in line abreast. They chugged toward the beach, slowly becoming visible to the enemy ashore, as night reluctantly gave way to the hazy gray dawn of a new day.

It was the morning of June 6, 1944. The beach was in Normandy, on the coast of France. The liberation of Europe had begun.

Sgt. John Slaughter of the 29th Infantry Division was on one of those Higgins boats that morning. He remembered: "It seemed like we were out there forever circling. I was trying to keep warm, trying to stay dry and trying to keep from throwing up. In the end I was throwing up into my own helmet, rinsing it in the bottom of the boat and throwing up again." But as the boats moved toward the shore, the motion and spray intensified. What really created a sensory overload, recalled Slaughter, was the firing of the heavy guns from the battleship _Texas_ to his starboard side. "BOOM-BA-BA-BOOM! BOOM-BA-BA-BOOM! The noise was just incredible," he remembered. "Each time she fired a salvo from her 14-inch guns the recoil squatted her down in the water, setting up a shock wave that would nearly swamp us. We were all sick, wet, miserable, bailing with our helmets, deaf from the guns, chilled from the wind and all I could think was 'Just get us in there. Nothing could be worse than this.'"[2]

In an allied fleet numbering hundreds of ships and thousands of smaller craft, the battleship _Texas_ was the centerpiece of the naval gunfire support for the invasion. The _Texas_ was the flagship for Rear Admiral Carleton Bryant, commander of the Fire Support Group, the ships and sailors responsible for providing accurate and effective naval gunfire to support the American troops involved in the amphibious assault.

But the _Texas_ was not one of the new, fast battleships sliding off the American shipbuilders' ways. Commissioned in 1914, the _Texas_ was an old and tired ship at the time of the American entry into

World War II. She had started life with great promise—to be one of the most powerful weapons in her country's arsenal. Because of advancing technology, changing tactics, and evolving world events, the *Texas* fell short of her early promise in the first few decades of her existence. By the time World War II began, a growing number of naval officers considered the *Texas* a throwback to an earlier age, an impediment in a new Navy centered on fast, powerful aircraft carriers. This is the story of how the *Texas* overcame early disappointments, avoided the scrap yards through continuous adaptation of mission and design, and ultimately fulfilled her destiny in World War II. She remains with us today as a testament to the growth of American sea power in the 20th century.

CHAPTER ONE

Birth of the *Texas*

From its very beginning, the United States has been a maritime nation, depending upon the sea for commerce and communication with other nations. In fact, one could argue that the precipitating event of the American Revolution occurred when the British closed Boston Harbor in 1774 in retaliation for the Boston Tea Party. As a result of being isolated geographically by vast oceans, the sea—and transportation on, and eventually over, the sea—has been and continues to be the life-blood of the nation.

The importance of sea commerce, and a navy to protect that commerce, is so great that the United States had a navy even before it was a country. On October 30, 1775, the First Continental Congress established the Continental Navy "for the protection and defense of the United Colonies" eight months before it declared independence from Great Britain.[1]

While the American Navy won several notable small engagements during the Revolutionary War—such as Capt. John Paul Jones in the *Bonhomme Richard* versus the British *Serapis*—it was never able to sweep the Royal Navy from the sea. The major function of the Continental Navy was to raid British commerce rather than attack the British Navy.

The tiny American navy, composed primarily of converted merchantmen, had an insignificant effect on the outcome of the war, and only one ship of the United States Navy, the *Alliance*, remained in commission when the Treaty of Paris ended the American Revolution in 1783.[2]

From 1785 until 1795 the United States had no navy at all, since Congress refused to fund a navy as an economic measure. But the seizure of American merchant ships and their crews by the Barbary pirates of Morocco, Tripoli, Algiers, and Tunisia made evident the need to have a blue-water navy to protect American commerce far from our shores. Congress resurrected the United States Navy, which experienced cycles of great strength and criminal neglect over the following years—years that included wars with Great Britain and Mexico, as well as the American Civil War.

In 1890 Capt. Alfred Thayer Mahan, an American naval strategist, historian, and lecturer at the Naval War College, profoundly changed the way the world viewed the sea. In his book *The Influence of Seapower Upon History, 1660-1783*, Captain Mahan argued that great nations are also great maritime powers. And they became great maritime powers by having great navies to protect their merchant fleets.

Mahan explained that for a country to be a great nation, to be economically and politically powerful, it must have a thriving and economically viable merchant fleet with which to conduct international trade. To protect the merchant fleet, the country must have a large and powerful navy. And to enable its navy to serve anywhere in the world in an age of coal-fired steam engines, a great nation must have overseas possessions to serve as coaling bases and supply and repair facilities. Therefore, a great nation must have a powerful fleet capable of long-range power projection, as well as imperial possessions in order to protect commerce. Mahan contended that a great navy must be composed of large, armored battleships, able to sail anywhere in the world, and fight decisive battles with any enemy.

Captain Mahan attracted great attention with his theories, and perhaps his greatest American adherent was the rising young politician Theodore Roosevelt. A young man keenly interested in the sea and naval affairs, at the age twenty-four Roosevelt wrote a book titled *The Naval War of 1812*. His interest in the navy and naval power continued, and he eventually had great influence on American naval affairs first as assistant secretary of the navy and later as the nation's youngest president.

It was President Theodore Roosevelt who persuaded a reluctant Congress to fund the creation of America's first world class navy, consisting largely of the armored battleships Captain Mahan advocated. At the direction of President Roosevelt the fleet of battleships, known as the Great White Fleet, sailed around the globe beginning in December 1908, in an unsurpassed display of naval might.

The United States was not alone in striving toward world naval supremacy. The island nation of the United Kingdom had long been the world's leading naval power and was not going to give up her position of supremacy lightly. In 1906, the Royal Navy commissioned a revolutionary new type of battleship—His Majesty's Ship (HMS) *Dreadnought*.

The *Dreadnought* had a main battery of ten 12-inch guns and carried heavy armor that protected the ship against guns of a similar size. Additionally, the ship had extremely powerful steam turbine engines that could propel the vessel at the then-amazing speed of 21 knots, or 24 miles per hour. With its large number of big guns, heavy armor, and high speed, the *Dreadnought* was more powerful than any other ship on the seas and faster than most.

The United States had actually begun construction of a *Dreadnought*-style battleship, the *South Carolina*, before the British began construction of the *Dreadnought*. But the British completed their ship faster than the U.S. completed the *South Carolina*, so the honor of leading the naval arms race went to the British. Which may be just as well, as *Dreadnought* has a much more militant, ominous sound than *South Carolina*.

President Theodore Roosevelt, ever the proponent of a powerful navy, urged the Congress to fund construction of more and more battleships. In some instances, he took an even more active role. In 1908, Roosevelt convened the Newport Conference, an assemblage of the major U.S. naval figures of the day, to discuss warship design and efficiency. One of the recommendations of the Newport Conference

America's newest battleship, U.S.S. Texas, *is launched.*

was to build new battleships with ten 14-inch guns. Previous American battleships had mounted 12-inch guns, but the British Royal Navy was then in the process of constructing 13.5-inch guns, and many naval architects thought the Germans were also working on weapons larger than their current 11-inch guns. The United States Navy wanted something bigger.

In January 1910, the newly designed 14-inch prototype was fired, and the results were better than anticipated. Therefore, the Navy's General Board decided that subsequent battleships would have the new 14-inch guns.[3] America's next battleship would become the most powerful weapon on the face of the earth.[4]

On June 24, 1910, the United States Congress authorized the construction of a new warship, battleship number thirty-five. In keeping with the tradition of naming battleships for states, the Secretary of the Navy decided to name the new ship for the state of Texas. The gov-

Miss Claudia Lyon, sponsor of the Texas, *prepares to christen the warship.*

ernment began accepting bids for the construction of the new ship on September 27, and the sealed bids were opened on December 1, 1910. Newport News Shipbuilding and Dry Dock Company of Newport News, Virginia, submitted the successful bid for the contract. The contract price for this newest battleship was $5,830,000, not counting the cost of armor and armament. The U.S. government and Newport News signed the contract for building the ship on December 17, 1910. The Navy delivered the plans and specifications for the ship to Newport News on December 24, and shortly thereafter the shipbuilding company ordered materials and began hiring construction crews.

The assembly of the warship began on April 17, 1911, with the laying of the ship's keel. Over the next weeks and months the building of the mighty ship progressed rapidly as workmen erected frames. Once the armor plate was received and installed, the ship began to take form. Workers fitted the massive rudder of the *Texas* on May 14, 1912, and in just a few days she was ready to take to the water.[5]

On May 18, 1912, only thirteen months after work began, the *Texas* was launched. In an impressive ceremony at Newport News, Virginia, Miss Claudia Lyon, daughter of prominent Texas Republican Cecil A. Lyon, christened the battleship with a bottle of champagne as it slid down the ways into the waters of the Chesapeake Bay. Attending Miss Lyon in her ceremonial duties was the daughter of President William Howard Taft and the daughter of Texas Gov. Oscar B. Colquitt.[6]

After the *Texas* was in the water, workers installed turrets, guns, and additional armor. The first turret went in on February 22, 1913, and on March 5 the first 14-inch gun took its place in the newest dreadnought.[7] Mechanics built the boilers and engines in place, deep within the cavernous bowels of the massive ship, while other laborers installed all the compartments and fixtures that made up a modern warship. Eventually workmen constructed the wooden main deck, and at last the contractor was ready to put the ship through her paces.

On October 23, 1913, a series of official trials began to determine if the new ship was ready to be accepted by the Navy. The first trial consisted of a series of thirty-four runs over a measured-mile course, beginning at the maximum speed of the ship and then at decreasing speeds down to ten knots. This trial determined that an engine speed of 124 revolutions per minute was required to attain the designed top speed of 21 knots (24 miles per hour), and 68 revolutions per minute to attain 12 knots (14 miles per hour).

The Texas *makes heavy smoke during her speed trials.*

On October 28, a four-hour full-speed trial began. The average speed for four hours was 21.05 knots, a little in excess of the designed speed. The next test was a twenty-four-hour coal and water consumption test at 12 knots, followed by a twenty-four-hour test at 19 knots. The final test was a two-hour trial in which the boilers burned coal and oil in combination. The results of the official trials were highly satisfactory, with the *Texas* slightly exceeding all design requirements.[8] After successful completion of the trials and attending to final construction details, the Newport News Shipbuilding and Dry Dock Company delivered the ship to the United States Navy at the Norfolk Navy Yard.

Thursday, March 12, 1914, was the big day—the day the United States Navy commissioned battleship *Texas* into service, joining the ship with the ranks of other battleships. A heavy snowfall lent a chilly holiday atmosphere to this otherwise somber and formal occasion. The ship was moored at the dock at the Norfolk Navy Yard, and during the morning the ship's crew of sailors, Marines, and officers filed

The crew marches aboard on commissioning day.

on board, marching past a horse-drawn Salvation Army wagon serving hot coffee. After coming aboard, the men formed on the starboard side aft, near the quarterdeck. Many of the crew had been staying on the U.S. Receiving Ship *Franklin* for several weeks, awaiting the day they would board their own ship—their new home.

Late in the morning visitors began to come aboard the *Texas* to witness the formal commissioning ceremony. At 12:30 P.M. Commander L.R. de Steiguer, acting commandant of the Norfolk Navy Yard, ordered the hoisting of the colors and then officially delivered the ship to her first commanding officer, Capt. Albert W. Grant. Captain Grant read to the crew and visiting dignitaries his orders from the secretary of the Navy, after which he delivered an address to his new crew. The brief ceremony lasted only five minutes, and then the crew was turned over to division officers and marched to quarters below decks and the watch was set. The *Texas* was no longer a ship under construction—it was the newest warship of the United States Navy.

The remainder of that day and the next several days were busy ones for the officers and enlisted crew of the *Texas*. As the galley was not yet operational, the crew had to go to the receiving ship for meals three times a day, going over by ship's boats and Navy Yard tugs. On the first trip back from dinner, the mid-day meal, the crew returned with seabags and hammocks, and saw that a lighter, or supply barge, filled with stores was waiting for them. As soon as they stowed their personal gear below decks, working parties received the stores from the lighter and from the docks.

Provisions and stores the crew brought aboard and stowed included foodstuffs necessary to feed the crew, as well as items to stock the ship's canteen. The first meal served on board the *Texas* was breakfast served at 7:30 A.M. on the 14th of March, and on Sunday the 15th Chaplain B.R. Patrick conducted the first divine service on board the ship.

On March 14, the paymaster brought aboard $5,000 in cash with which to pay the crew and various expenses. For the next several days, new crew members, officers as well as enlisted men, sailors as well as Marines, reported aboard periodically. The size of the initial crew grew, and each new member joined in the efforts to get the ship ready for sea. While the crew labored to receive and stow the provisions and stores, the officers were busy with inspections and receiving visitors from other ships. Everyone wanted to see the newest battleship and to pay respects to her captain.

On Tuesday, March 17, an ammunition barge came alongside, and the officer of the deck of the *Texas* hoisted the powder flag for the first time, indicating that gunpowder was being brought aboard the ship. The crew then received and stowed 304 rounds of 3-pounder saluting ammunition, 3,400 pounds of black powder, 1,095 primers, 2,000 hair-felt wads, and 2,000 cork wads for the saluting guns.

Even after the *Texas* was commissioned laborers from Newport News Shipbuilding and Dry Dock Company continued working on the ship, laying linoleum and finishing up other minor details. Additionally, shipfitters, joiners, caulkers, riveters, plumbers, and other workers from the Navy Yard remained on board completing various tasks and correcting problems discovered by the crew.

Provisions for the U.S.S. *Texas*, March 1914

FOOD ITEMS: 1,710 pounds of bread, 1,420 pounds of turnips, 390 pounds of carrots, 25,200 pounds of potatoes, 150 dozen eggs, 288 pounds of chipped beef, 300 pounds of buckwheat, 300 pounds of barley, 483 pounds of dried lima beans, 490 pounds of hominy grits, 400 pounds of cornstarch, 500 pounds of kidney beans, 225 pounds of currants, 90 pounds of hops, 648 pounds of rolled oats, 459 pounds of oyster crackers, 576 pounds of corn meal, 550 pounds of fish, 1603 pounds of butter, and 60 pounds of compressed yeast.

SUPPLIES FOR THE CANTEEN (Ship's Store): six dozen pipes, 288 pipe mounts, 2,000 packages of cigarette papers, 3,000 cans of tobacco for pipes and cigarettes, 1,100 pounds of Star chewing tobacco, 700 packages of playing cards, 504 packages of salted peanuts, 1,000 tins of sardines, 1,500 packages of maple walnuts, 1,500 packages of peanut brittle, 144 jars of peanut putter, 1,500 packages of chocolates, 1,000 packages of mixed chocolates, 240 bottles of mustard, 240 bottles of sweet pickles, 252 bottles of sour pickles, 144 bottles of catsup, 36 boxes of soap, 48 shaving brushes, 36 boxes of shoe polish, 72 tins of Shinola shoe polish, 144 tins of talcum powder, 144 tooth brushes, 144 pairs of garters, 504 blue handkerchiefs, 48 boxes of 3-in-1 oil, 60 cans of blanco, 60 boxes of silicone, 1,500 cakes of Ivory soap, 1,000 cakes of Naptha, 1,000 cakes of Lava, 1,600 cakes Life Buoy, 48 mirrors, 500 pairs of gloves, 500 pairs of shoe laces, 2 gross clay pipes, 1 gross dental cream, 1 gross dental powder, 8 dozen cakes of shaving soap, 8 dozen boxes of shaving powder, 500 bath towels, 500 wash cloths, and 620 sets of sweat clothes for physical training, and 96 padlocks.

SOURCE: U.S.S. *Texas* Log Book, March 1914.

A sailors most dreaded job—coaling ship.

The most disagreeable job a sailor had to perform in the Navy during the age of steam was loading coal onto the ship (known as "coaling ship"). The boilers of a battleship had voracious appetites and consumed enormous amounts of coal. Replenishing the coal supply was a filthy, backbreaking job, and that job began on the morning of April 19. The Navy Yard tug *Mohawk* brought a lighter or small barge alongside the *Texas* and at 5:30 in the morning the crew prepared to coal ship. A working party went into the lighter and shoveled coal into large canvas bags that other men then hoisted by crane onto the deck of the *Texas*. Some sailors dumped the bags out onto the deck, while others shoveled the coal into wheelbarrows and then dumped the coal into chutes leading down to the coal-bunkers on the third deck. In just over an hour the working party took on board 53 tons of coal. After a brief halt for breakfast, coaling continued until 2:30 in the afternoon, by which time 281 tons of coal had been taken aboard. While part of the crew was coaling ship, other sailors brought on board a more ominous and war-like cargo, consisting of twenty 14-inch shells and forty 5-inch shells.[9]

The *Texas* was a massive and powerful warship—beautiful to behold, and the pinnacle of battleship design and development. When commissioned in 1914 the ship was the most powerful weapon on the face of the earth, a testimony to the men who designed and built her.

The *Texas* was 573 feet and ¾ of an inch long and 95 feet and 2⅝ inches wide. The ship's designed load water line (draft) was 28½ feet from the bottom of the keel, and the depth from the keel to the main deck amidships, was 48 feet, 8¼ inches. Her freeboard or distance from the water line to the main deck amidships was 20 feet, 3⅝ inches. The highest point on the ship, the truck light on top of the cage mast, was 140 feet above the water line. Her normal load of fuel was 1,900 tons of coal and 267 tons of oil, although the ship could hold a maximum capacity of 2,891 tons of coal and 400 tons of oil. Her displacement with a normal load was 27,000 tons. The vessel was built with 141 longitudinal frames numbered fore to aft, spaced 4 feet apart.[10]

The three decks that ran the entire length of the ship were the main deck, the gun deck (second deck), and the protective and berth deck (third deck). There was a half-deck forward that ran from frame 1 to frame 25 between the gun deck and the berth deck. The half-deck was the berthing area for junior officers and warrant officers. Below the protective and berth deck were two platforms, or decks that were interrupted and did not run the entire length of the ship. The boiler rooms and engine spaces interrupted the platforms. Below the second platform were the hold and the inner bottom.[11]

The primary reason for the existence of the *Texas*, as for that of any battleship, was her main battery. The design and operation of the ship revolved around the big guns. As historian Theodore C. Mason explained in his excellent book *Battleship Sailor*: "From the lowliest mess attendant to the captain himself, everyone was in the service of the guns. All the machinery and equipment the men operated, all the braid and chevrons and regimentation, were dedicated to one task: loading, elevating, and training the gargantuan rifle barrels, so that they would speak with tongues of orange flame and shattering sound, hurling projectiles across the horizon in lofty, decaying curves to descend upon, penetrate, and destroy the ships of the enemy."[12]

The main battery of the *Texas* consisted of ten guns, known as 14-inch, 45-caliber breech loading rifles. The guns fired a shell 14 inches in diameter, making them the largest guns afloat in any navy. The bore of the gun, 14 inches, was called its caliber. The length of the barrels was expressed in multiples of the caliber, so the barrels were 45 times the bore, or 45 calibers long. Thus the barrels were 45 times 14 inches, or 630 inches (52½ feet) long. The 14-inch guns were mounted in pairs in five electrically controlled turrets on the centerline of the ship. There were two turrets forward and three turrets aft. The turrets numbered one through five, from the forwardmost turret aft.[13]

The guns were loaded from the breech, or rear, as opposed to the old muzzle-loading types of cannon used in the Civil War. The fact that the guns are rifled indicates that the bore is cut systematically in a spiral pattern beginning at the powder chamber at the breech and extending to the muzzle. The cut portions of the barrel are called the grooves, while the raised portions of the barrel between the grooves are called lands. This system of lands and grooves is known as rifling. When a projectile is fired a soft copper driving band or rotating band fixed to the shell is forced into the groove, and when propelled forward, imparts a twist or spin to the projectile. This enables the pro-

Cannisters containing cloth powderbags for the 14-inch guns.

jectile to fly much farther and much more accurately than if the gun barrel were smooth, in which case the shell would tumble end over end resulting in decreased accuracy.

The ammunition for the big guns did not come with the projectile and propellant enclosed together as is the case with modern small arms ammunition. The powder charge for the 14-inch guns came in silk cloth bags that the gunners placed in the gun behind the projectile. A separate primer placed in the breechblock then ignited the propellant and caused the gun to fire.

Raw silk was used for the construction of the powder bags because after firing a gun, silk left fewer residues of ash and burning embers in the breech than other fabrics did. The large grains of gunpowder were stacked on end in rows in the bags, layer upon layer. After the powder was placed in the bags, they were sewn up with silk thread and tightly laced with a silk cord. The end result was a very stiff, compact powder bag weighing 105 pounds.

The large grains of smokeless powder used in the 14-inch powder bags were difficult to ignite, so an ignition charge had to be used. The ignition charge was made by enclosing the proper amount of black

The powderbags were stored in metal cans or tanks, similar to these.

powder in a very fine silk bag, then quilting the sides of the bag together to form the ignition pad. Black powder was used because it ignites rapidly and gives off an intense flame. The face of the ignition pad is made of silk cloth dyed red, so an observer could tell at a glance that it was the ignition end. The ignition pad was then sewn to the bottom of the bag with the red face on the outside of the end of the bag. The other end of the powder bag was fitted with a handling strap. This strap was used to withdraw the bag from its container, the powder tank and for handling the bag while loading the gun.[14]

Setting off or igniting the black powder ignition charge itself required a primer. The primer is a small brass tube open on one end and closed on the other, containing 40 grains of very fine black powder. The closed end of the primer holds a small cap containing fulminate of mercury, a highly explosive substance. The explosion of this cap ignites the black powder primer. Either percussion or the application of an electrical current can activate the cap, and so the primer is called a combination lock primer.[15]

Before the powder bags were placed in the guns they were kept in airtight containers known as powder tanks. The powder tanks were

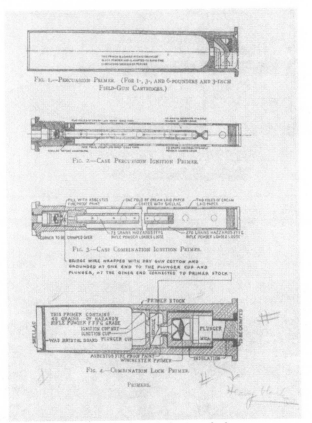

This primer ignited the powderbags.

made of sheet steel, copper, or aluminum, and each tank contained two powder bags.[16]

There were two main types of projectiles used in the 14-inch guns: armor piercing and high capacity. The armor piercing or AP shell was designed to penetrate the heavy face-hardened armor plate that protected battleships. The point of the armor-piercing projectile is extremely hard and well tempered to enable it to penetrate armor plate. Over the tempered point of the shell is a blunt protective cap of soft steel. When the projectile strikes an armored surface, the soft steel cap is crushed down around the tempered point of the projectile, supporting the point as it pierces the armor plate. The soft steel cap also reduces the possibility of the shell glancing off the armor plate. A 14-inch armor piercing shell from the *Texas* could penetrate

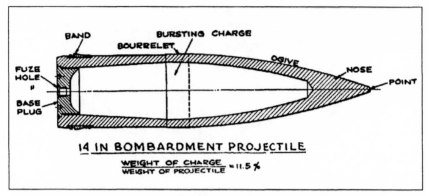

Drawing of a high-capacity shell.

14-inch shells on the main deck of the Texas.

an armor plate 16 inches thick at a distance of nine thousand yards, or a little over five miles.

The early 14-inch armor piercing shells weighed 1,400 pounds and contained a bursting charge of 31½ pounds of explosive. The explosive was either dunnite, known as "Explosive D," or trinitro-toluene (TNT). To detonate the bursting charge, a detonating delayed-action fuse was inserted in the base of the projectile. This type of fuse ensured that the shell did not explode on impact with an armor plate, but rather after it had penetrated the armor plate.[17]

Main battery of the USS Texas.
14-inch gun turrets atop their armored barbettes.

The two portside torpedo tubes are visible below the
water line in this photo.

Sailors man a 5-inch gun.

The other main type of 14-inch projectile used on the *Texas* was the high-capacity shell. These shells were designed for use against unarmored targets such as smaller ships and targets ashore and therefore did not need to be built so ruggedly. The outer case of the projectile needed to be only strong enough to withstand the shock of firing, so they could have a greater cavity and hold more explosive.[18] A 14-inch high-capacity shell weighed 1,275 pounds and had a bursting charge of 147 pounds.[19]

In addition to her main battery of 14-inch guns, the *Texas* also had four 21-inch Mark I submerged torpedo tubes, two on each side of the ship. The tubes were located in the forward part of the ship between frames 31 and 36, well below the water line. The torpedoes were fired from the submerged tubes by a charge of compressed air. The *Texas* initially carried twelve torpedoes manufactured by E.W. Bliss and Company. Designed by Frank Leavitt, the torpedoes were known as Bliss-Leavitt Mark III torpedoes. Each torpedo was 21 inches in diameter and 5 meters—or about 16 feet, 5 inches—long. Compressed air powered the turbine engines of the torpedoes, which had a practical range of 4,000 yards and a speed of at least 27 knots or nautical miles per hour.[20]

The *Texas* had an impressive secondary battery in addition to the 14-inch guns. It consisted of twenty-one 5-inch, 51-caliber rapid-firing guns. Nineteen of the guns were mounted on the gun deck (one deck below the main deck) with the remaining two being mounted on the superstructure deck (one deck above the main deck) just aft of the number two turret. One of the guns was mounted on the centerline at the stern of the ship on the gun deck and was known as the "stinger." Initially the *Texas* also had four 3-pounder saluting guns, two 1-pounder boat guns, one 3-inch field gun, and two 30-caliber machine guns.[21]

As a battleship in the *Dreadnought*-style and era, the *Texas* was of course heavily armored. The main belt side armor extended from frame 18 to frame 137. Between frames 18 and 122 the armor was 12 inches thick at the top and tapered to 10 inches thick at the bottom. From frame 122 aft to frame 137 the armor was 6 inches thick. The main belt side armor was 7 feet 11½ inches from top to bottom, with the top of the belt 23½ inches above the designed normal load water line. Therefore, the heaviest armor was from about two feet above the water line to about six feet below the water line, the area where incoming enemy shells had the greatest potential to sink the ship. Above the main belt side armor was the lower casemate side armor, extending upward to the bottom of the 5-inch gunport sills. This armor was 11 inches thick at the bottom and tapered to 9 inches thick at the top. The upper casemate side armor extended upward to the top of the 5-inch gunport sills and was 6½ inches thick.

The main battery turrets and the barbettes upon which they sit were also heavily armored.[22] The face of the turrets were 14 inches thick, while the front portion of the sides of the turrets were 9 inches thick, and the rear portions of the side were 8 inches thick. The rear of each turret was also 8 inches thick, while the roof plates of the turrets were 4 inches thick. The barbettes were generally 12 inches thick, tapering to 10 inches on the areas facing amidships. The side walls of the conning tower armor were 12 inches thick, while the top plate or roof of the armored conning tower consisted of 8 inches of armor.[23]

Two of the decks of the ship boasted some armor protection as well. The protective deck, or third deck, had armor from 1½ to 3 inches thick. The second deck, or gun deck, had armor of only ½ inch.[24]

The power to move the massive battleship came from two engines built inside the ship by Newport News Shipbuilding and Dry Dock Company. Each was a vertical inverted, direct acting, 4-cylinder triple expansion engine. Each engine had a high-pressure cylinder 39 inches in diameter, an intermediate-pressure cylinder 63 inches in diameter, and two low-pressure cylinders 82 inches in diameter. Each engine turned outboard, and the length of the stroke of each cylinder was 48 inches. The two engines were in separate engine rooms and were mirror images of each other. At a speed of 124 revolutions per minute, the two engines combined produced 28,000 horsepower.[25] The *Texas* had twin screws, or propellers, with each engine being connected directly without gearing to a single brass propeller. Each propeller had three blades and was 18 feet 7¾ inches in diameter. The pitch of each propeller was 19 feet 11½ inches. This meant that theoretically each time the propeller made one revolution, the ship moved forward 19 feet 11½ inches.

Providing the steam for the engines were 14 coal-fired water-tube boilers built by Babcock and Wilcox, a firm specializing in boilers. The boilers were in four separate watertight compartments. Each boiler was 17 feet 2½ inches long, 9 feet 7 inches wide, and 12 feet and ⅞ of an inch tall.[26]

Of course all the hardware described above was only useless steel without a skilled and courageous crew to man the ship. The initial crew of the *Texas* consisted of about 950 officers and enlisted men, including about 75 Marines. Her first captain was Albert W. Grant, who graduated from the U.S. Naval Academy in 1877. After serving on the U.S.S. *Massachusetts* at the Battle of Santiago Bay during the Spanish-American War, Grant worked his way up through the ranks to become Chief of Staff of the Atlantic Fleet before commanding the *Texas*, the newest and most powerful ship in the world. Captain Grant and his crew were anxious to prove themselves and their new ship worthy of the trust their nation placed in them.

CHAPTER TWO

Early Years and "Over There:" The *Texas* in World War I

The *Texas* did not have the benefit of the usual shakedown cruise and lengthy post-shakedown repair period of a newly commissioned warship. In February 1913, Mexican Army Gen. Victoriano Huerta led a coup that ousted Mexican President Francisco Madero. General Huerta or his followers then murdered the deposed president and vice president, enraging U.S. President-elect Woodrow Wilson, who took office in March 1913. President Wilson refused to grant diplomatic recognition to the Huerta government and sent U.S. warships into Mexican waters to protest the actions of General Huerta and protect American interests in the country.

More than a year after the coup, on April 6, 1914, a landing crew from the U.S.S. *Dolphin* was loading supplies at a dock in Tampico, Mexico, when General Huerta's soldiers arrested seven sailors and the ship's paymaster and placed them in jail. A senior officer of the Mexican Army soon released the Americans, but the American naval commander at the scene, Rear Admiral Henry T. Mayo, demanded a formal apology and a 21-gun salute to the American flag. General Huerta refused. President Wilson asked Congress for authorization to

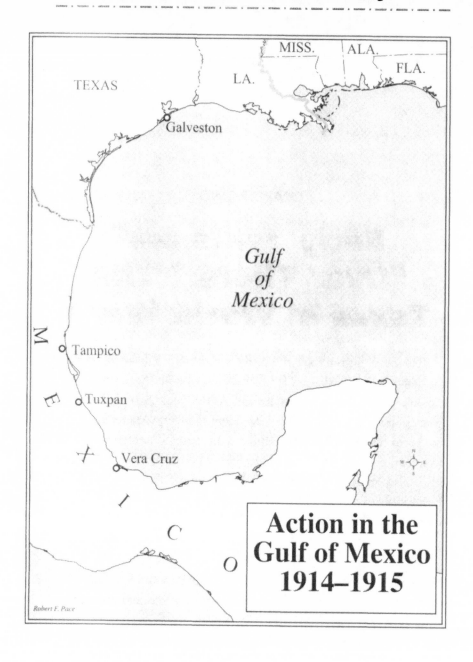

MISS. ALA.

FLA.

TEXAS LA.

Galveston

Gulf of Mexico

M
E
X
I
C
O

Tampico

Tuxpan

Vera Cruz

Action in the Gulf of Mexico 1914–1915

Robert F. Pace

The U.S.S. Texas *at Vera Cruz in April 1914.*

use force to compel respect for the American flag, and Congress consented.

On April 21, 1914, American Marines and bluejackets, or sailors, under the command of Rear Admiral Frank Friday Fletcher landed at the Mexican port city of Vera Cruz and quickly occupied the port and major portions of the city. In three days of fighting seventeen sailors and five Marines were killed, and seventy Americans were wounded. For a time, it seemed as if there would be a full-scale war between the United States and Mexico.[1]

The crew of the _Texas_ attended a memorial service in New York on May 12, 1914, for the Marines and sailors killed in the battle at Vera Cruz. The funeral procession marched up Broadway to City Hall, where five hundred school children took part in the ceremony honoring the dead. The procession then marched to the Brooklyn Barracks in the New York Navy Yard for the funeral service. President Woodrow Wilson and Vice President William Jennings Bryan were among those at the service, and the Marines of the _Texas_ fired three volleys to honor the dead during the ceremony. On May 15, 1914, the _Texas_ departed the New York Navy Yard and joined the American forces in Mexican waters, dropping anchor at Vera Cruz on May 23. The ship remained in the area for just over two months, departing on August 8 and returning to the New York Navy Yard on August 21.[2]

After the conclusion of the occupation of Vera Cruz, the *Texas* joined the Atlantic Fleet and settled into a routine of normal fleet operations. During this time the ship participated in training operations, tactical exercises, and gunnery drills. It returned to the Mexican coast in October 1914 and became the station ship at Tuxpan, Mexico, for a few weeks, then interrupted her Mexican patrol for an enjoyable interlude in early November.

Leaving the Mexican coastal town of Tuxpan behind on November 4, the dreadnought sailed for the port city of Galveston, Texas, arriving there on November 6, 1914. For several days the crew enjoyed the hospitality ashore, while many citizens from Texas came to view and tour "their" battleship. A highlight of the ship's visit to Texas occurred on November 7 when Gov. Oscar Colquitt presented a magnificent silver service to Captain Grant. The Young Men's Business League of Waco, Texas, raised the necessary ten thousand dollars and donated the silver to the officers and men of the battleship. Among other gifts showered on the crew was a black bear cub, named Ursa, presented to the crew as a mascot by the Texas Company, an emerging oil company later known as Texaco.[3]

After enjoying abundant shore leave for several days, the crew returned to their ship and resumed their naval duties. The *Texas* said farewell to Galveston on November 14 and sailed for Tampico, Mexico, and then on to Vera Cruz for a month. The ship finally departed Mexican waters on December 20 and returned to the New York Navy Yard, staying there for repairs from December 28 until February 16, 1915.[4] After rejoining the Atlantic Fleet, the *Texas* resumed the normal peacetime training schedule.

The vessel broke from this routine on May 25, 1915, when at four in the morning the ship received an urgent radio message that a steamer was in distress about fifty miles away. The *Texas*—along with the battleships *South Carolina*, *Louisiana*, and *Michigan*—responded to the call. The Norwegian fruit steamer *Joseph J. Cueno* had rammed

Presentation of the ship's silver in Galveston.

the Holland-America Line passenger ship *Ryndam* south of Nantucket Shoals, off the coast of Rhode Island. The *Texas* raced to the scene at top speed, and with other ships helped rescue 230 passengers, including thirty-two women and ten children. No lives were lost in the accident or rescue operation. The *Texas* then escorted the damaged liner during a nineteen-hour voyage to the Holland-American dock in New York's North River.[5] The Holland-America Line presented the *Texas* with a silver and pewter replica of the seventeenth-century Dutch ship *De Zeven Provincien*, the flagship of Admiral De Ruijiters from April 1666 to October 1674, a time when the Dutch were a premier maritime nation.[6]

In June 1914 a European nobleman, of whom most Americans had never heard, was shot in a country most Americans couldn't find on a map. Archduke Franz Ferdinand, heir to the throne of Austria-Hungary, was visiting Sarajevo when political terrorists assassinated him. The murder of Archduke Franz Ferdinand and the political bumbling that followed erupted into war between the most populous and most powerful nations in Europe. The Central Powers, composed primarily of Austria-Hungary and Germany, confronted the Allied Powers, led by Russia, France, and Great Britain. In August 1914, diplomacy failed to resolve the trouble between the two belligerent factions, and Germany invaded Belgium and France. Soon millions of young men were fighting and killing each other along European battlefronts that stretched for hundreds of miles. The First World War had begun.

During the first years of the massive conflict, the United States remained neutral, not openly taking sides with either the Central Powers or the Allies. Although it was not fighting, the United States Navy was closely following the war and paying attention to the lessons learned by the belligerents. One such lesson involved airplanes.

The battleship *Texas* was designed in 1910, and at that time airplanes and the danger they posed to battleships were not a factor in ship design. Airplanes of the day were considered novelties, little more than expensive toys really, and certainly not a threat to a capital ship. Naval planners in the United States noted the effectiveness of the airplane as a weapon in the early years of World War I, however, and moved to counter the new threat. In July 1916 the *Texas* installed two 3-inch, 50-caliber guns atop her boat-crane derrick posts, and became the first battleship of the American Navy to have anti-aircraft guns.[7]

Very early in the conflict, German surface ships and submarines began to prey on the merchant ships supplying food, arms, and supplies to England and France. Merchant ships carrying goods to Europe began arming themselves with guns to repel the assaults of the submarines, which often attacked while surfaced. This counter-threat to German submarines, also called U-boats for undersea boats, led German ships to attack surface ships without prior notice. Attacking civilian merchant ships, as well as civilian passenger liners, led to great loss of civilian life, and the United States government considered such action an outrage.

The final road to American intervention in the Great War began on January 31, 1917, when the German ambassador notified the United States Government that Imperial Germany would begin an

The 3-inch sky gun, or anti-aircraft gun.

unrestricted submarine campaign in the area surrounding the British Isles. In seeking to starve the island nation into submission, the Germans proposed to sink every ship—British, allied, or neutral—found in British waters. On February 3, 1917, President Woodrow Wilson recalled the American ambassador from Berlin and ordered the German ambassador to leave the United States. On April 6, 1917, the United States Congress declared that a state of war existed between the United States and the Imperial German Government.

Immediately after the declaration of war, President Wilson sent a naval delegation to England to confer with their British counterparts and work on a comprehensive naval war plan for the two countries. According to Rear Admiral William Sowden Sims, the leader of the American delegation, the most pressing need of the Royal Navy was more destroyers to assist in detecting and hunting down the submarines that operated in the waters surrounding Great Britain. Sending American destroyers across the Atlantic contradicted American Naval policy of keeping the fleet intact, and the Navy Department in Washington resisted the idea. Naval planners in Washington believed that the United States should keep the U.S. fleet together and await a decisive confrontation with the enemy before dispersing the fleet. This plan did not take into consideration the fact that the German High Seas Fleet was effectively bottled up in harbor by the British Grand Fleet. Eventually the Navy Department relented and sent a number of U.S. destroyers to the British Isles to assist in the anti-submarine campaign.

The Royal Navy, with a limited pool of trained officers and seamen, proposed to decommission several older battleships and use their crews to man new destroyers if the United States would send battleships to replace the decommissioned British ships. In November 1917, Secretary of the Navy Josephus Daniels decided to send a division of older, coal-burning battleships to augment the British fleet instead of the newer oil-burning ships; Britain had plenty of coal with which to fuel the ships, but no indigenous oil supply.[8]

With the declaration of war, training on the *Texas* intensified. In addition to her own crew, the *Texas* also trained gun crews for service aboard merchant ships. The Navy Department made the decision to arm merchant ships with deck guns, often taking 5-inch guns from older battleships and placing them on the steamers to enable them to protect themselves from submarines and surface raiders. Naval gun crews manned the guns on the merchant ships.

During the fall of 1917 the *Texas* went to the New York Navy Yard for a routine overhaul. While she was in the yard, rumors abounded that several American battleships would join their allies in the British fleet, and the crew of the *Texas* hoped they would soon be on their way to Europe.

In late September the *Texas* departed the New York Navy Yard and headed up the coast of New York to enter the Long Island Sound. While sailing at night the ship ran without any lights, in respect for the German submarine menace. During the early morning hours of September 27, 1917, Capt. Victor Blue and the navigator, Commander Frank Martin, were on the bridge. To enter Long Island Sound the ship had to turn near Block Island, off the coast of Rhode Island, while avoiding an extensive minefield in the area. In the pitch-black darkness, the captain and navigator miscalculated when to turn the ship and ran hard aground onto Block Island.

The ship was grounded from the bow all the way back to aft of the boat cranes, well beyond the middle of the ship. The *Texas* was fully loaded with fuel, ammunition, and stores. The crew off-loaded ammunition, anchors and chain, the coal from the fuel bunkers, and other movable items in an effort to make the *Texas* lighter, so she could float free of the island.

While the outer hull had been pierced in many places, the inner hull of the double bottom was intact. Naval architects and engineers from the New York Navy Yard arrived on the scene to assist in the recovery, and yard workers installed air compressors and forced the water out of some of the flooded compartments. For three days the ship was stuck on the island, and finally tugboats pulled her free. During the efforts to move the *Texas*, the crew of her sister-ship, the *New York*, chanted, "Come on, *Texas*," giving the *Texas* the motto she carried throughout her service life.[9]

The grounding severely damaged the hull of the *Texas*, and the ship was forced into dry dock at the New York Navy Yard for repairs. There she remained from October 4 until December 5, 1917. During that time yard workers repaired the punctured hull, and removed three of the 5-inch guns, one on each side amidships, and the "stinger" in the stern of the ship. While the *Texas* was in the Navy Yard undergoing repairs and modifications, the other American dreadnoughts of Battleship Division 9 sailed across the Atlantic to join the British fleet in November. The *Texas* was left behind.[10]

Once repairs were complete, the *Texas* left dry dock and engaged in a series of exercises to test her seaworthiness. While participating in maneuvers at sea on January 15, 1918, the ship lost three men who were swept overboard during a heavy squall. One man was rescued, but the other two perished. Their bodies were never recovered.[11]

During the various maneuvers at sea the battleship fleet learned many lessons. One was that the 5-inch gun ports on the sides of the ships were too near the water line and consequently very wet and shipped water in even a moderately rough sea. Capt. Victor Blue later wrote that during the war only four guns were manned while the ship was at sea. These were the two 5-inch guns on the superstructure deck and the two 3-inch guns on the boat crane posts. The two forward 5-inch guns on each side, mounted in the officers' ward room, were practically useless as a result of taking on water, as was the "stinger," the gun mounted in the very stern of the ship. On January 27, 1918, workers at the New York Navy Yard removed the forward-most guns, and plated over their ports.[12]

Once repairs were complete and the vessel was fit for duty, the *Texas* departed from New York on January 30, 1918, and set sail for the British Isles. After an eleven-day trip across the stormy North Atlantic, the *Texas* picked up an escort of three British warships on the morning of February 11. The *Texas* followed her guides to the massive Royal Navy base at Scapa Flow, in the Orkney Islands north of Scotland. There she joined the *New York, Wyoming, Florida,* and *Delaware,* the other American dreadnoughts that comprised the Sixth Battle Squadron of the British Grand Fleet.[13]

Once the *Texas* was safely in harbor, the crew expected a few days of rest and relaxation after the arduous Atlantic crossing, which was an endurance test for men and ship alike. Heavy seas and pounding waves destroyed several of the ship's boats during the voyage. Rest for the weary crew had to be postponed, however, as a collier pulled up alongside the ship only a few hours after the ship dropped anchor. The men of the *Texas* spent their first night with the Grand Fleet coaling their ship. The arduous task began late in the afternoon of Monday, February 11 and continued throughout the night until 11:00 the next morning. The crew spent the remainder of the day cleaning up the filthy mess made by the coal dust.

After completing a "field day," or thorough cleaning of the ship, the newly arrived sailors finally had a chance to catch up on rest, reading, and letter writing. Their leisure was interrupted at 1:00 in the morning of Saturday, February 16 when the ship received orders to prepare to sail. Following almost immediately after the first message came additional orders to "expedite," and "clear ship for action." In less than two hours the *Texas,* along with the remainder of the Sixth

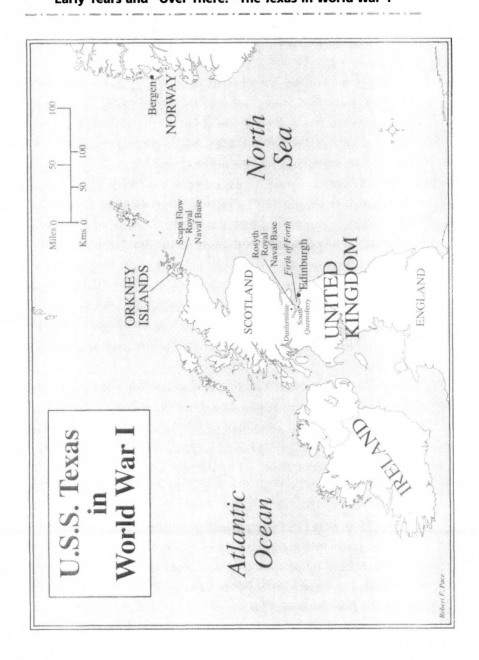

Battle Squadron and the five British squadrons, was under way and moving out to sea.

Once at sea the battleships went to general quarters. Crewmen secured all watertight doors and hatches and manned all the ship's guns. Unknown to the men of the *Texas*, the British Admiralty had received word that the German High Seas Fleet had put to sea, and the Grand Fleet moved to intercept the enemy.

After the sun came up over the storm-tossed North Sea, the *Texas* sailed along with the other battlewagons. When the ships ahead of her suddenly swung out of line, lookouts on the *Texas* spotted a submarine periscope one thousand yards away on the port bow. The crew of the number twenty 5-inch gun fired one shot at the periscope, after which several destroyers raced to the spot and immediately began dropping depth charges. The submarine disappeared, no more to be seen. Although the number twenty 5-inch gun did not hit the U-boat, it did have the distinction of firing the first combat shot from the *Texas*.

After hunting for the German ships for more than a day, the Grand Fleet returned to Scapa Flow. After the war it was discovered that the two fleets had come within forty miles of each other, but the decisive fleet engagement so strongly desired by the British and Americans never took place. The Germans had discovered that the Grand Fleet was looking for them, and the German Navy did not want to risk a major sea battle. Eluding the Grand Fleet, the German High Seas Fleet safely returned to its harbors. The fact that the *Texas*, the newest arrival among the dreadnoughts, was prepared for a major fleet action only four days after arriving overseas made a favorable impression with the remainder of the fleet—especially among the British counterparts.[14]

Arriving back at the fleet anchorage of Scapa Flow, the sailors of the *Texas* engaged in what became a dreaded but necessary routine: coal ship and then field day the ship. Coaling ship was necessary to keep the fuel bunkers full because the Grand Fleet could be ordered to sea at any time, while the field day was necessary to keep the ship neat, tidy, and in fighting trim.

During the vessel's service with the Grand Fleet the *Texas* spent much of the time training to master the skills necessary in warfare. Much of the training centered on the various guns of the ship. The 5-inch guns, for close defense, fired torpedo defense practice at ranges from five thousand to over eight thousand yards, or two and a half to four miles. The 14-inch guns naturally fired at longer ranges, from ten thousand to twelve thousand yards, or five to six miles.

The *Texas* broke from training routine on March 7 when she and the other ships of the American squadron received orders to escort a convoy to Norway. The squadron, along with a group of British destroyers, left anchorage during the early morning hours of March 8 and sailed into the North Sea, where they met up with a convoy of thirty merchant ships bound for Bergen, Norway. After delivering the merchantmen safely to their port, the dreadnoughts of the Sixth Battle Squadron returned to their berths in Scapa Flow.[15]

A change of scenery lay in store for the *Texas* when the ship received orders on Thursday, April 8 to make preparations for getting underway. After standing out to sea, the ships of the Grand Fleet received word that they were all bound for the British naval base of Rosyth, in the Firth of Forth, near Edinburgh, Scotland. Arriving there on April 12, the sailors from the *Texas* thought they might be once again near civilization, compared to the bleak wasteland of Scapa Flow. Any thoughts of going ashore, however, had to wait until after the now-customary ritual of coaling ship followed by a field day. After the crew attended to these duties, many of the Texas sailors went ashore to take in the sights of South Queensferry and Dunferline, quaint little villages near the anchorage. While the larger city of Edinburgh was off limits, the men enjoyed their time visiting the Scottish lassies in the tiny towns.

On April 17 the *Texas* weighed anchor and put to sea on another convoy trip to Norway. As the Sixth Battle Squadron and its destroyer escort sailed to intercept the convoy, lookouts spotted a submarine periscope just as a torpedo passed between two of the American dreadnoughts. Gunners on the *Texas* fired two 5-inch shots at the submarine, and destroyers rushed to the scene, dropping depth charges. The submarine disappeared, its fate uncertain. The *Texas* and the other warships sailed on to Norway and picked up a convoy of forty-eight merchant steamers. After safely shepherding the convoy back to England, the escorts returned to Rosyth in the Firth of Forth on April 20. Four days later the *Texas* and the other ships of the Grand Fleet again sortied out from their anchorage. The German High Seas Fleet had dashed out from Jade Bay toward the Norwegian coast in an attempt to intercept an Allied convoy. Forward elements of the two fleets came within sight of each other, but at extreme ranges, and once again the Germans refused to be drawn into an engagement. The High Seas Fleet returned to its base on April 25, and the Grand Fleet followed suit the following day.[16]

The month of May passed quietly for the men of the *Texas*, who enjoyed their new naval base in the Firth of Forth. All hands received ample liberty, and many of the officers and men traveled to Edinburgh to take in the sights. Training continued, with emphasis placed on gunnery and maneuvering to avoid torpedoes. The *Texas* experimented with a new innovation in warfare in May when the ship received a kite balloon. The balloon, attached to the *Texas* by a cable and telephone line, carried two observers eight hundred to one thousand feet above the ship. From their elevated vantage point, the observers could seek out enemy ships and correct the fall of shot of friendly ships.[17]

On June 9 the dreadnoughts of the Sixth Battle Squadron built up steam and got underway. Heading north, the *Texas* and her squadron mates returned to their former base at Scapa Flow. Once more settled into the familiar but desolate anchorage, the ships began a schedule of gunnery practice, fleet maneuvers, normal maintenance, and coaling ship. The training routine was broken on Sunday, June 30 when the Sixth Battle Squadron put to sea to protect U.S. and British mine-laying ships sewing their deadly cargo in the North Sea between Scotland and Norway. The North Sea mine barrier made it extremely difficult for German U-boats, or submarines, to enter the North Atlantic.[18]

It was not all work and no play for the sailors of the *Texas* while in foreign waters. While in Rosyth several members of the crew set out

Assistant Secretary of the Navy and future president, Franklin D. Roosevelt on the Texas.

to put together a first-class baseball team. The practice games showed promise, and in their first contest with another ship the *Texas* team defeated the *Delaware* by a score of nine to one. Following this lopsided victory, the *Texas* challenged all the other battleships, and baseball games became the rage in Forsyth. The undefeated record of the *Texas* held until a second game with the team from the *Florida*, in which three of the *Texas* starters did not play. The last game of the Sixth Battle Squadron championship was against the *Wyoming*, and the *Texas* nine once again proved victorious. The *Texas* team then went on the road, defeating two Army teams in England before coming up against a headquarters team from London. The London team had five professional baseball players as well as several minor league stars, and they were too much for the *Texas* team. Despite this defeat at the hands of a more or less professional team, Admiral Hugh Rodman declared the *Texas* team champion of the Grand Fleet, with a record of eight wins and two losses.[19]

Several distinguished visitors came aboard the *Texas* while she was in British waters. Admiral Hugh Rodman, commander of the Sixth Battle Squadron, came aboard several times for inspections and consultations with Capt. Victor Blue. Other visitors included Assistant Secretary of the Navy (and future president) Franklin D. Roosevelt, Admiral Mayo, and Lord Jellicoe, First Lord of the British Admiralty.[20]

During the summer and fall of 1918, the *Texas* and her squadron-mates continually trained for a battle that never took place. The squadron moved back and forth from Scapa Flow to the Firth of Forth, occasionally dashing out to sea in an attempt to intercept German ships, but never taking part in a ship-to-ship or fleet-to-fleet duel with the enemy. A brief stay in a floating dry dock at Newcastle-on-Tyne provided an interesting interlude, and on November 4 the *Texas* left the dry dock and returned to the Firth of Forth. By this time rumors were circulating of the imminent surrender of Germany, and Captain Blue reminded the men of his ship that a naval battle could still take place at any time.

On November 11, 1918, Germany finally surrendered, and the Grand Fleet celebrated with wild abandon. Sailors cheered and danced, searchlights pierced the night sky, and colored rockets streaked across the heavens as the crew of the *Texas*, and people everywhere, gave thanks for the end of the war. On November 20 Admiral David Beatty, commander of the Grand Fleet, directed that the fleet would stand out to sea the following day to accept the surrender of the German High Seas Fleet. The *Texas* took her place in the battle line and along with the other battleships, battlecruisers, cruisers, and destroyers of the Grand Fleet, met the surrendering ships of the German High Seas Fleet about forty miles east of May Island in the North Sea. As the fleets met, the American and British ships formed a double column, with the German ships in between. The Grand Fleet thus escorted its docile captives back to Scapa Flow and internment. After enjoying a Thanksgiving Day feast as guests of the British sailors of the Fourth Battle Squadron, the *Texas* sailed to Portland, England, arriving there on December 4.[21]

On December 12 the *Texas*, along with other American ships, met President Woodrow Wilson, who was sailing to Europe in the naval transport U.S.S. *George Washington*. The *Texas* and the other ships escorted the president to Brest, France, arriving there on December 13.

On the following day the *Texas* took on board three airplanes, as well as a large number of passengers, primarily Army officers seeking passage home.

At 2:00 P.M. on December 14, 1918, the *Texas*, along with other American battleships, departed France and set a course for home. The Sixth Battle Squadron returned to New York on Christmas Day 1918, but Navy officials did not allow the ships to enter the harbor until the following day. Secretary of the Navy Josephus Daniels wanted to review the fleet as it came into the Port of New York, and Daniels was unable to come to the harbor until the day after Christmas. The delay infuriated many of the sailors, who had to spend Christmas Day on board the ship, within sight of land but unable to go ashore to spend the holiday with their families. On December 26, New York City paid tribute to the officers and men of the Sixth Battle Fleet, who for more than a year stood ready and willing to battle the German foe. Hundreds of small craft in the harbor escorted and saluted the American warships, and crowds cheered the men as they came ashore.[22]

During the Great War, later known as World War I, the *Texas* and her crew did not fight any heroic battles, pitting great fleets against each other. The German fleet seldom went to sea during the last year of the war and never offered to fight the British Grand Fleet, augmented as it was with American reinforcements. While this lack of action might indicate the *Texas* and her sister ships did not serve a useful purpose, the opposite is actually true. The *Texas* and the other American battleships tipped the balance of naval superiority so far in favor of the British Fleet that the German Navy made a conscious decision to not seek battle. The *Texas* and her crew contributed greatly to winning the war by simply being a threat, a potent force in readiness, able and prepared to destroy the German High Seas Fleet if it ever left the safety of its harbors. The *Texas* protected the United States, while achieving an incredible bloodless victory over a dangerous German Navy.

CHAPTER THREE

An Interlude of Peace

After the First World War, the *Texas* became a part of Battleship Division Six, along with *Arkansas, Mississippi,* and *New York,* on duty with the Atlantic Fleet. Capt. Nathan C. Twining, who took command of the *Texas* on December 31, 1918, had been an Annapolis classmate of Capt. William V. Pratt of the *New York* and Capt. Louis de Steiguer of the *Arkansas.* The Commander of Battleship Division Six was Rear Admiral Hugh Rodman, flying his two-star flag above the *New York.*[1]

One of the many technological innovations to be used in a military manner during the Great War was the airplane. A relatively new invention, being first flown by the Wright brothers in 1903, the airplane, or aeroplane, was first considered a novelty or a rich man's toy. During the course of the war, however, the combatants discovered they could put machine guns on the flimsy aircraft, and even use them to drop bombs on enemy troops or towns. One of the most important aspects of the airplane, however, was its great potential as a reconnaissance vehicle.

In the days before aerial observation, the crew of a battleship could only see as far as a man in the mast could look with his eyes. His vision might be enhanced with optical devices such as binoculars, but even so his line of sight was limited by the horizon. No matter how great the magnification of a lookout's optics, he could not see over the horizon. The airplane changed that. Even in the days before adequate portable radios, an airplane could fly great distances, locate an enemy fleet or other targets, and relay that information to friendly ships via written messages dropped from the cockpit. With the advent of reliable radios, of course, communication was much easier.

During the World War, navies experimented with balloons tethered by cables to ships to augment the observation capabilities of the ships. The *Texas* received her first observation balloon on May 28, 1918, while anchored at the Firth of Forth in Scotland. Whenever a squadron of four to six battleships went to sea on maneuvers, at least one ship towed an observation balloon, also known as a kite balloon. The dreadnoughts towed the balloons at a height of eight hundred to one thousand feet, and each balloon carried two observers in a small basket. These observers had telephone communications with the bridge of the towing ship, augmenting the lookouts in the mast.[2]

During the war the Royal Navy had gone a step further and experimented with flying airplanes from ships that served as aerial reconnaissance platforms. American naval officers had great interest in the British experiments, and the crew of the *Texas* actually built a small runway platform above and attached to the number two turret while the ship was in dry dock at Newcastle-on-Tyne in October 1918. The record is not clear, but an airplane may have been put aboard the *Texas* at that time, but if so, the aircraft was not flown before the end of the war. That milestone occurred a few months later.[3]

In March 1919, while in Guantanamo Bay, Cuba, the *Texas* became the first United States battleship to launch an airplane. Lt. Commander Edward O. McDonnell flew a British-built Sopwith Camel from the flying-off platform erected over turret two on March 9. The ship was stationary, at anchor, at the time of the launch, so the pilot did not have the benefit of the ship's speed to help him to get airborne. The Sopwith Camel was so light, however, that it was able to take off without crashing, and the experiment was a success. After taking off from the ship, the airplane participated in a main-battery gun exercise, where the pilot spotted the fall of the shot from the 14-inch guns. Captain Twining was very favorably impressed with the

A Sopwith Camel on turret two.

accuracy of the spotting and encouraged the Navy to further develop the concept. The airplane flown from the *Texas* had no provision for landing either on the ship or in the water nearby, so it had to land on a conventional runway at the Guantanamo Naval Base. While the use of airplanes assigned to ships aroused some interest in their scouting abilities, the true value of naval airpower and its appreciation was still some years in the future.[4]

In May 1919 the *Texas* had a further experience with naval aviation. Air power proponents within the Navy planned to fly across the Atlantic Ocean. The airplane chosen for the voyage was made by a young aviation construction pioneer named Glenn Curtis, and the plane he built was called the Navy Curtis, or NC. The plane, often referred to as a flying boat, was a seaplane, designed to land on and take off from the water.

One of the planners of the trans-Atlantic flight was Commander Richard Byrd, who designed aerial navigation instruments specifically for this mission. Navigation for the flight was particularly difficult, as there would be no land references for a pilot to determine his location. Commander Richard Byrd, a graduate of the U.S. Naval Academy, later gained fame as the great polar explorer.

Four Navy seaplanes, NC-1 through NC-4, began the expedition at Naval Air Station Rockaway, New York, on May 8, 1919. Only one aircraft, NC-4, successfully completed the journey, landing in Portugal on May 27. The *Texas* was one of dozens of U.S. Navy vessels that supported the operation. Ships lined the entire route of the flight, with a vessel stationed every fifty miles across the ocean. These support ships assisted the planes with their navigation and relayed weather information to the pilots.

During the summer of 1919 the crew of the *Texas* said goodbye to the east coast as the dreadnought transferred to the Pacific Fleet. Going through the still-new Panama Canal was an exhilarating experience for the sailors and an opportunity to see one of the great marvels of the twentieth century. The following year, on July 17, 1920, the Navy redesignated the *Texas* as BB-35. This new naming resulted from the adoption of the alpha-numeric hull designation. The *Texas* served in the Pacific until 1924, at which time she returned to the east coast for a routine overhaul, followed by a training cruise to Europe.[5]

The United States had begun an ambitious and expensive battleship construction program in 1916 and the building of the great ships continued after the World War ended. Japan, an emerging naval power, had also embarked on a vast construction project to increase the size and quality of its navy. The leaders of Great Britain, the island nation completely dependent upon the sea for its survival, felt that their country must have a navy at least as large as any other navy, so Britain also continued to build battleships.

When President Warren G. Harding moved into the White House in 1921, he found that he had inherited a naval arms race. The United States, Japan, and Great Britain were spending themselves into the poorhouse, and President Harding became determined to stop the unnecessary expenditure of funds. At the direction of the president, Secretary of State Charles Evans Hughes invited representatives from the naval powers of the world to meet in Washington, D.C. in November 1921 for naval arms negotiations. Great Britain, Japan, France, and Italy responded.[6]

The negotiations concluded with the signing of the Washington Naval Treaty on February 6, 1922. The treaty limited the total tonnage of capital ships to the following displacements: United States, 525,000 tons; British Empire, 525,000 tons; Japan, 315,000 tons; France, 175,000 tons; and Italy, 175,000 tons. This gave the naval powers a capital ship ratio of roughly 5:5:3:2:2. The treaty also stipulated that the displacement of capital ships could not exceed 35,000 tons each, and guns could not exceed 16 inches in caliber. The agreement also limited the size and number of aircraft carriers and cruisers, and it defined capital ships as those in excess of 10,000 tons displacement or carrying guns with a caliber larger than 8 inches.

This treaty, which successfully ended an international arms race, limited the number of battleships in the United States Navy to eighteen. No new battleships would be built for the next fifteen years.[7] Instead of being scrapped and replaced with newer ships, older ships such as the *Texas* would need to be upgraded and have their service lives extended. Modifications would include replacing the coal-fired boilers with oil-fired boilers, addition of anti-torpedo blisters, and addition of armor to the decks to protect the ship from aerial attack.

In April 1922, two months after the signing of the Washington Naval Treaty, the Navy's General Board recommended that the *Texas*, along with the other older battleships *New York*, *Wyoming*, *Arkansas*, *Utah*, and *Florida*, undergo extensive modifications. The oldest ships would go in first. The *Texas* had to await her turn for modernization.[8]

On December 6, 1922, Secretary of the Navy Edwin Denby issued General Order Number 94 that formally altered the fleet names and command arrangements. Previously there had been two major divisions, the Pacific Fleet and the Atlantic Fleet. Under the new order, the Pacific Fleet was renamed the Battle Fleet, and, along with the Fleet Base Force, would operate in the Pacific Ocean. The Atlantic Fleet became the Scouting Fleet and would operate from the east coast. The combined fleets made up the United States Fleet. The

Battle Fleet contained twelve battleships, while the Scouting Fleet had six. Within the Battle Fleet were Battleship Division Three (*New York*, *Texas*, *Oklahoma*, and *Nevada*), Battleship Division Four (*Pennsylvania*, *Arizona*, *Mississippi*, and *Idaho*), and Battleship Division Five (*New Mexico*, *Tennessee*, *Maryland*, and *California*). The commander of the three battleship divisions was Vice Admiral Henry A. Wiley in the *New Mexico*. The *Texas* was a part of the Battle Fleet, based in San Pedro, California. During the next two years the *Texas* conducted routine peacetime training exercises, until returning to the east coast in 1924. In that year the ship embarked a group of Naval Academy midshipmen for a training cruise to European waters, after which she conducted maneuvers as an element of the Scouting Fleet.[9] The naval experience of the Great War exposed some glaring weaknesses in the battleships of the great navies. The Battle of Jutland, for instance, showed clearly that the deck armor of capital ships was inadequate and needed to be strengthened. Since the Washington Naval Treaty of 1922 precluded the building of new battleships to incorporate the lessons learned from the World War, the existing battleships of the United States Navy would have to be modified and improved. To that end the battleship *Texas* entered the Norfolk Navy Yard on the first day of August 1925 for a major overhaul and extensive modifications. The vessel remained in the yard until November 23, 1926.[10]

During the year and four months the ship was in the yard, the *Texas* was largely rebuilt. Construction workers removed much of her superstructure and main deck in order to make massive internal modifications. The Washington Naval Treaty did not address the propulsion of existing battleships, so that was a major area of renovation. As originally built the *Texas* had fourteen coal-fired boilers in four separate compartments. The Navy determined that all the U.S. battleships should use the same fuel, so workers at the Navy Yard removed the old boilers and replaced them with six new oil-fired boilers in three watertight boiler rooms. These new boilers were originally built for *South Dakota*-class ships that had been cancelled as a result of the treaty.[11] A highly visible modification related to the boilers was the reduction of number of stacks, or smokestacks, from two to one.

The change from coal-fired to oil-fired boilers meant that there was much more usable internal space in the ship, as oil took up less space than coal. As a result, workers modified spaces alongside the hull on the third deck that had previously been used for coal storage to become crew berthing areas. The renovations also called for additional bulkheads installed below the third deck in the oil storage tanks. These bulkheads increased the underwater protection from torpedoes by adding an extra compartment shielding the vital boiler and engine rooms of the ship.

The *Texas* had been designed and built with two underwater torpedo tubes on each side of the ship. As the ranges for effective gunfire increased, the use of torpedoes as offensive weapons by a battleship became increasingly unlikely. During the major overhaul the workers removed the torpedo tubes and plated over the holes in the hull.

Modifications such as the removal of the torpedo tubes and the reduction of boiler rooms from four to three meant that there was more internal space available along the centerline of the ship. Naval architects made good use of this space by adding a naval gunfire plotting room, part of the new gunfire control systems installed at this time. Additionally, the *Texas* added an internal communications and electrical distribution room, and a large radio room.

The Washington Naval Treaty of 1922 was specific about modifications to the armor and armament of capital ships. The old dreadnoughts could not be reconstructed except for the purpose of providing means of defense against air and submarine attack, and those modifications were limited to an increase of three thousand tons displacement for each ship. Anti-torpedo blisters could be added to the outside of ships, and deck armor could be increased, but not to exceed the specified weight limits. Alterations to the side armor or the main armament of the battleships were prohibited.[12]

One of the major deficiencies of battleships discovered during the Great War was that their armor was insufficient to withstand plunging shells fired from great distances. These shells struck the decks of battleships, rather than the heavily armored sides. The weakness of the deck armor was all the more glaring when paired with the realization that airplanes could be used as offensive weapons and could drop bombs onto ships. To compensate for this weakness the Navy increased the armor on two decks of the ship—the berthing and protective deck, or third deck, as well as the gun deck, or second deck. The Navy increased the second deck armor to 4½ inches in the area between number two turret and number five turret, while increasing the third deck armor to 3 inches.

To better protect the ship from torpedoes, the navy yard added anti-torpedo bulges, or blisters, on the outside of the hull. These blisters increased the width or beam of the ship from 95 feet, 2⅜ inches to 106 feet. The blisters were designed as simply a void, or dead-air space, that could absorb the impact of a torpedo and keep the explosion away from the ship's hull. The blisters could also be flooded as an emergency measure, if necessary.

One of the most visible alterations to the mighty dreadnought was a change in masts. The *Texas* had been built with two cage-type masts that resembled tall, cylindrical wicker baskets. Experience showed that the cage masts whipped in the wind and could not support any significant weight. So new, heavier, tripod masts replaced the old, light cage masts. The mainmast, nearest the middle of the ship, moved farther aft, and the foremast became the home of a relocated chart house and a new pilot house or navigation bridge. Workers built a new fire control center for the main and secondary batteries at the top of the foremast and a secondary fire control center into a new tower just aft of the stack.

On November 23, 1926, the newly rebuilt *Texas* left the Norfolk Navy Yard and went to sea. For the next few weeks, the ship experienced an intensive shakedown period to grow accustomed to the changes and discover any problems resulting from the refit. After more modifications, including the addition of a flag bridge above the navigation bridge, the *Texas* rejoined the fleet as the flagship of the United States Navy.

The *Texas* gained one of her more colorful characters when Admiral Henry A. Wiley became commander-in-chief of the United States Fleet in 1927. Admiral Wiley was born in Pike County,

Alabama, in 1867, and his family moved to McKinney, in Collin County, Texas, when Wiley was less than a year old. He grew up in McKinney and considered Texas his home. Wiley entered the United States Naval Academy on April 16, 1883, and graduated in June 1888. After a steady progression in the Navy, including command of the battleship division and duties in Washington, D.C., Admiral Wiley earned the top sea-going post in the Navy.

In 1927 the flagship _Texas_ was stationed at San Pedro, California. On the morning of November 8, 1927, all the flag officers and captains at the harbor came aboard the _Texas_, and at ten o'clock in the morning the ship's bugler sounded attention. Admiral C.F. Hughes relinquished command of the fleet, after which Admiral Wiley read his orders naming himself as commander-in-chief. Admiral Wiley relieved Admiral Hughes, and Admiral Hughes ordered his four-star flag to come down. The ship's band played the Admiral's March, and the ship's guns fired a salute of seventeen shots. Then Admiral Wiley ordered his flag run up, and the band and the saluting guns repeated their performances. The visiting officers went back to their ships, Admiral Hughes went ashore, and the United States Fleet had a new commander-in-chief.

Wiley's tenure was almost a very brief one. Darkness descended as the _Texas_ was underway in the channel headed out to the open sea, and the new commander-in-chief went out on the pitch-black deck to observe the navigation. While walking about on the forecastle of the yet-unfamiliar ship, Admiral Wiley fell down the hawse-pipe, the hole on the side of the deck through which the anchor chain passed. While slipping through the pipe, the admiral grabbed onto the shank of the anchor and clung for dear life. The admiral's assistant chief of staff, Captain Anderson, heard the admiral's cries for help and pulled him back up onto the deck. Admiral Wiley was cut and bruised, his uniform torn and covered with fresh paint from the anchor. A very close call for the first day on the job![13]

Capt. Joseph R. Defrees assumed command of the _Texas_ on January 4, 1928, and shortly thereafter the ship served as host for a most distinguished visitor. Havana, Cuba, held the Pan American

Congress that year, and the battlewagon had the honor of transporting President Calvin Coolidge and his party to the occasion. After completion of an overhaul in New York, the *Texas* sailed to Key West, Florida in January 1928. There she picked up President and Mrs. Coolidge, Secretary of State and Mrs. Frank B. Kellogg, Secretary of the Navy and Mrs. Curtis Wilbur, and numerous other officials, aides, Secret Service agents, and reporters.

Owing to the lack of depth at the Key West Harbor, the *Texas* had to anchor five miles out from the dock. President Coolidge and his group boarded the cruiser *Memphis* and then transferred over to a tug before they could come aboard the *Texas*. In spite of heavy seas and foul weather, the transfer occurred without mishap and the *Texas* sailed across the Florida Straits to Cuba.

As the battleship neared Morro Castle, the Cubans fired salutes, and ships in Havana Harbor blew their whistles. When the *Texas* anchored, a number of Cuban dignitaries came aboard to welcome the president to their island nation, then President Coolidge and the official party went ashore for the opening of the Pan American Congress the next day.

In order to avoid a transfer between ships in the open sea again, the president decided to return home in the *Memphis*. In the early morning hours of January 17, President Coolidge departed Cuba and returned to Key West, with the *Texas* escorting. Upon their arrival at Key West, the *Texas* fired a twenty-one gun salute and sailed for Haiti.[14]

Being the flagship of the United States Fleet imposed additional burdens on the crew of the *Texas*. There was always a restrained, almost tense feeling about the ship. The captain of the ship never really had the ability to conduct his own affairs, and those of his men, as he saw fit. In the back of his mind, the captain always knew an admiral was looking over his shoulder. The commander-in-chief of the U.S. Fleet was responsible for supervising fleets in both the Atlantic and Pacific, as well as showing the flag to friendly countries, and his flagship was always on the go.

But being a flagship had its rewards as well. While most ships of the fleet were stuck in port, the *Texas* was steaming and sailing to many parts of the world. Many ships left port in the morning, conducted drills during the day, and returned to port in the evening, staying in their home port for at least nine months out of the year, venturing out only once for the annual fleet problem. But not the *Texas*. It was part of the duties of the commander-in-chief of the U.S. Fleet to show the flag and spread goodwill, but Admiral Wiley, in particular, had another reason for keeping the *Texas* cruising. He contended that a ship kept at sea, visiting many different ports, had a better trained, more experienced, and happier crew than one that stayed at a home port three-quarters of the year.

After leaving President Coolidge in Key West, the *Texas* sailed to Haiti to observe the operations and exercises of the Scouting Fleet. The flagship arrived at Port-au-Prince, and local dignitaries welcomed and entertained the admiral and other officers. The admiral and captain of the *Texas* responded by hosting a tea and dance for the president of Haiti on board the battleship.[15]

The *Texas* next dropped anchor at Guantanamo Bay, Cuba. The Scouting Fleet, or Atlantic Fleet, had concentrated at Guantanamo for training and annual target practice. The *Texas* departed Guantanamo Bay and steamed for the British Colony of Kingston, Jamaica, for a good-will port call. For the next three days the British governor, Sir Reginald Stubbs, and the commander of the British North Atlantic Squadron, Admiral Sir Walter Cowan, entertained Admiral Wiley and the officers of the *Texas*.[16]

After departing from Kingston Harbor on February 6, the *Texas* returned to Guantanamo Bay. On the 8th, crewmembers of the *Texas* observed an airplane circle the ship and dip its wings in salute. The pilot was Charles Lindbergh, on his first flight to Cuba. The stay in Cuba was short, and on February 9 the *Texas* weighed anchor and sailed for New Orleans, where the crew of the ship represented the Navy in the annual Mardi-Gras festivities. It was undoubtedly a most enjoyable time for officers and crewmembers alike.[17]

Admiral Wiley concluded his career at sea and hauled down his flag from the mast of the *Texas* on May 21, 1929. On that day

Admiral Wiley turned over the United States Fleet to Admiral William Veazie Pratt.[18]

Admiral Pratt, as commander-in-chief, United States Fleet (CinCUS), broke out his flag on the *Texas* and moved aboard the fleet flagship. He had been a Naval Academy classmate of a previous captain of the *Texas*. Capt. Nathan C. Twining, captain of the *Texas* from December 1918 until July 1919, and Admiral Pratt were both in the Naval Academy class of 1889.[19] Admiral Pratt had scarcely taken up his residence on the flagship before the *Texas* went into the New York Navy Yard for its annual overhaul, where it stayed most of the summer. After the overhaul, as the home and headquarters of the CinCUS, the ship spent most of its time at port in Brooklyn, Boston, Newport, or Annapolis.[20]

Admiral Pratt assumed command of the United States Fleet at a financially difficult time. Congress had never voted the funds necessary to give the Navy a well-balanced fleet in accordance with the Washington Naval Treaty of 1922. While the United States had the battleships necessary to fulfill the 5:5:3 ratio with Great Britain and Japan, the Navy was short of cruisers and other combat auxiliaries. Getting the needed funding from Congress to balance the fleet became more difficult after the onset of the Great Depression in October 1929.

An interesting highlight of Admiral Pratt's tenure as commander-in-chief was his reception and hosting of a Japanese delegation to the United States. Kichisaburo Nomura had been the Japanese naval aide in Washington during the World War, and Nomura and Admiral Pratt had been friends since that time. In September 1929, Vice Admiral Nomura brought the Japanese Navy Training Squadron to the United States. On September 27, Admiral Pratt invited Admiral Nomura and his staff aboard the *Texas* and entertained them on the flagship. Admiral Pratt had on his staff a Japanese cook, who prepared a sumptuous meal for the distinguished Japanese visitor.[21] More than a decade later, Admiral Nomura became the Japanese Ambassador to the United States in November 1940 and arrived in Washington in February 1941 in an effort to improve relations between the two countries. Admiral Nomura was still in Washington, ostensibly negotiating for peace, when Japan attacked Pearl Harbor on December 7, 1941.[22]

Born in 1869 in Belfast, Maine, William Veazie Pratt came from a seafaring family and was naturally drawn to the sea. He entered the United States Naval Academy in 1885 and graduated in 1889. In September 1929 Admiral Pratt was able to fulfill a childhood dream when he sailed his flagship *Texas* into Penobscot Bay, the harbor of his hometown.[23] It was an accomplishment very few men could achieve.

Admiral Pratt, however, soon moved on to other assignments. The London Naval Conference convened in January 1930, and President Herbert Hoover ordered Admiral Pratt to be a member of the delegation. Chief of Naval Operations Charles F. Hughes appointed Admiral Louis M. Nulton as acting commander-in-chief, United States Fleet. Admiral Nulton moved up from commander, Battleship Fleet, on January 9, 1930. Admiral Nulton commanded the United States Fleet during the annual winter maneuvers in the Caribbean, the largest annual exercise of the United States Navy.[24]

The *Texas* left the New York Navy Yard in January 1931 after a routine overhaul and once again assumed the mantle as flagship of the United States Fleet. She crossed through the Panama Canal and headed for San Diego, the ship's home for the next six years. After serving as flagship for the U.S. Fleet, the *Texas* became flagship for Battleship Division 1. During the summer of 1936, the vessel briefly returned to the Atlantic to participate in a midshipman training cruise. After the cruise, she immediately returned to the Pacific and the Battle Force.[25]

In the summer of 1937, the *Texas* returned to the East Coast and became flagship of the Training Detachment, United States Fleet. In late 1938 or early 1939, the *Texas* became flagship of the Atlantic Squadron, a newly organized unit built around Battleship Division 5. Her primary duties in this capacity were in training sailors, midshipman cruises, and training members of the Fleet Marine Force.[26] By this time many naval observers considered the *Texas* an aging ship past her prime. What they did not know was that her greatest challenges, and her greatest contributions, lay ahead.

CHAPTER FOUR

The War Begins

During the 1930s world events began taking an ominous turn. In September 1931, the Empire of Japan sent an army to occupy the Chinese region of Manchuria, after which the Japanese government quickly declared that Manchuria was independent of China, and Japan installed a ruler for the newly created country. Adolph Hitler became chancellor of Germany in January 1933, and later that year both Germany and Japan withdrew from the League of Nations. In December 1934, Japan renounced the Washington Naval Treaty, opening the way for Japan to begin a naval arms buildup. The following year, Germany announced it had an air force and was building submarines or U-boats, in direct violation of the Versailles Treaty which ended the First World War. In 1937, renewed fighting between Japanese and Chinese forces in China broadened the Asian conflict, and Adolph Hitler abrogated all terms of the Versailles Treaty.[1]

Throughout this time of world crisis, the United States, suffering economically from the results of the Great Depression, maintained a policy of isolationism, refusing to be drawn into world affairs. Great Britain and France, also enduring economic hardships, lacked the political will and military might to intervene in the affairs of Germany and Japan without the support of the United States, thus encouraging the rogue nations to continue their expansionist doctrines.

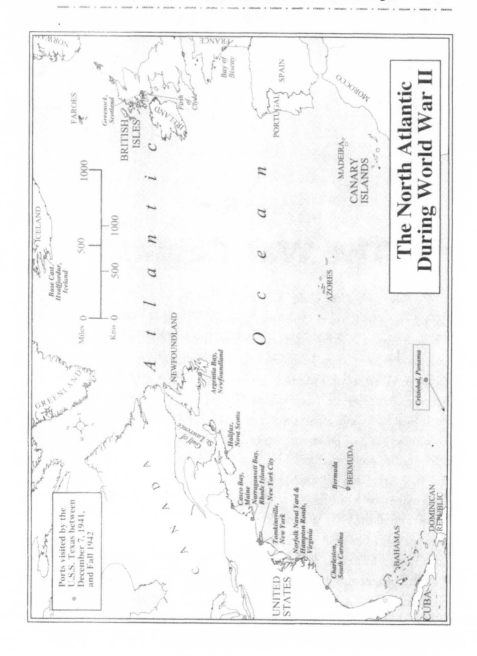

The North Atlantic During World War II

In the late 1930s the countdown to war continued. Germany annexed Austria in March 1938, which had the effect of making Austria a part of Germany. In a morally indefensible move, in September 1938 British Prime Minister Neville Chamberlain met with Hitler and offered to give to Hitler a portion of Czechoslovakia in exchange for Hitler's promise of peace. After dismembering the central European country, Chamberlain returned to England proclaiming he had achieved "peace for our time." The peace lasted less than a year. Once Hitler had gobbled up what remained of Czechoslovakia, without interference from the United States, Great Britain, or France, his German Army invaded Poland on September 1, 1939. The brutal assault on a peaceful, neighboring country, without even the benefit of a declaration of war, finally awoke the leaders of civilized nations and forced them to recognize that Adolph Hitler was an aggressive, duplicitous dictator without regard for international law and intent on conquering his neighbors, if not the world. On September 3, Great Britain, France, Australia, and New Zealand declared war on Germany.

The next several months were not kind to the Allied Powers, principally Great Britain and France, and their dominions overseas. The Axis Powers—Germany, Italy, and Japan—continued victorious on all fronts. German forces conquered western Poland quickly, while the Soviets (who had signed a non-aggression pact with Hitler) moved rapidly into Latvia, Lithuania, Estonia, and eastern Poland. Britain and France frantically prepared for war. Germany invaded Denmark and Norway in April 1940 and had moved into Belgium, Holland, and France by May. The elevation of Winston Churchill to Prime Minister was a boost to British morale and aggressiveness, but the Allied forces were unable to halt the German advances into the low countries of Western Europe. By May 26, British expeditionary forces in France began evacuating across the beaches at Dunkirk, and on June 22 France surrendered to Germany.

Upon the outbreak of the war in Europe, the United States declared its neutrality and on September 12, 1939, began naval patrols out into the Atlantic Ocean to keep the belligerent navies out of American waters. The *Texas* was one of the ships involved in these "neutrality patrols."

During the interval between the eruption of war in Europe on September 3, 1939, and the attack on the United States Fleet at Pearl Harbor more than two years later, the United States Navy and Marine Corps spent the time wisely preparing for war. In early 1940 the *Texas*, under the command of Capt. Clarence Hinkamp, participated in a major amphibious exercise at the island of Vieques in Puerto Rico. The *Texas* provided gunfire support for Marines who stormed ashore in a mock attack on the beach. Afterwards, many high-ranking officers who participated in the exercise came aboard the battleship to critique the operation. Admiral Ernest J. King, Commander in Chief of the Atlantic Fleet, flew his flag over the *Texas*. Also attending the post-battle critique were Marine Maj. Gen. Holland M. Smith and Secretary of the Navy Frank Knox.

Fireman Third Class F.R. Smith had just come off watch from the dynamo condenser room and had taken a shower in the engineer's shower room in the starboard passageway on the second deck. Momentarily forgetting about the gathering of flag officers on the ship, Smith playfully threw a bucket of water on a shipmate and fled from the shower room. He ran forward to the athwartship passageway, turned left, and headed for the port passageway. He then turned left, headed aft, still running at full speed. As he turned the corner he ran into the protruding belly of Secretary of the Navy Frank Knox, who was coming forward down the port passageway! Mr. Knox grunted and threw up his hands. Right behind the Navy Secretary was Admiral King, followed by General Smith and other flag officers. At the end of the gold-braided procession was the captain of the *Texas*. Fireman Smith, scared out of his mind, froze at attention against the bulkhead, clad only in a towel and carrying a bucket. Each high-ranking officer glared menacingly at the young sailor as they continued on their way forward to the wardroom. None of the officers spoke a word.

After the incident, Fireman Smith hurried to his compartment and got dressed. He waited in his compartment, fully expecting the master-at-arms to come arrest him at any moment. No one ever mentioned the incident. The brass probably found the incident amusing after the initial shock, but Fireman Smith lived in terror for the next several days.[2]

During the remainder of the year, the *Texas* and her crew continued with "neutrality patrols," interspersed with routine peacetime training, although the training had taken on a greater sense of urgency as a result of the wars being fought in Europe and Asia. During the first months of the war the U.S. maintained strict neutrality, but as time progressed and it became increasingly clear that Germany was the aggressor nation in the war, the U.S. attitude changed. Under the leadership of President Franklin D. Roosevelt, America began giving more active support to the Allied cause, convoying ships carrying Lend-Lease material to Great Britain.

During 1941 the *Texas* made several trips across the Atlantic, escorting merchant ships out to a mid-Atlantic meeting point where the convoy met a British naval escort that then took the convoy on to England. On June 20, 1941, during one of these Atlantic voyages, the German submarine U-203 stalked the *Texas* for several hours and sent a radio message to U-boat headquarters in Germany requesting permission to attack the dreadnought. But naval commanders in Germany denied permission to attack the American battleship, not wanting to provoke the U.S. into declaring war on Germany at that time.

In early 1941 a momentous event occurred on the deck of the *Texas* while she was in the waters off Puerto Rico. On February 1, 1941, the 1st Marine Division was formally activated on the quarterdeck of the *Texas*. Maj. Gen. Holland M. Smith was the first commanding officer of the division, the first unit of that size in the history of the Marine Corps. Two subsequent commanding generals of the division, Maj. Gen. Pedro del Valle and Maj. Gen. Oliver P. Smith, had served with the Marine Detachment on the *Texas* earlier in their careers. The 1st Marine Division covered itself in glory during World War II, first at Guadalcanal, then at Peleliu and Okinawa, and continues to serve our nation well into the twenty-first century.

By the middle of October 1941, the new home port of the *Texas* was the U.S. Naval Base in Argentia, Newfoundland, in Canada. While in port at this temporary base, the captain made his weekly Saturday inspections of the crew and living spaces, and shore patrol units went ashore for routine temporary duty at Roche Point, Argentia, Newfoundland. The officer of the deck made daily inspections of the magazines and tested smokeless powder samples. The ship's airplanes and aviation crew kept busy with flights almost every day, sometimes twice each day. Gasoline for the aircraft and fuel oil for the ship's boilers was replenished and ammunition was taken aboard.

Exercises continued while the *Texas* was in her Canadian port. Tuesday, November 11, 1941, was a fairly typical day. During the early morning hours the *Texas* fired up her boilers and made preparations for getting underway. At 7:03 A.M. the ship weighed anchor and got underway to conduct engineering trials. Getting underway included energizing the degaussing circuits as a precaution against magnetic mines and streaming the paravanes to protect the ship against anchored mines. As the depth of the water increased to more than one hundred fathoms, or six hundred feet, the degaussing circuits were de-energized and the paravanes recovered, as the danger from mines decreased with the depth of the ocean.

After the ship reached the open sea, various steering controls were exercised. While sailing at a speed of fifteen knots, steering control using the electric steering motor was shifted from the bridge to the central station, a more protected area inside the ship on the third deck, directly below the armored conning tower. After a few minutes the steering control was shifted to the armored conning tower itself. Then the bridge resumed the steering control and shifted over from electric steering to steam steering, using the steam-powered steering engine to turn the rudder, rather than the electric motor. Control of the steering was then shifted to the trick wheel, located in the rear of the engine room. Then steam steering control was shifted to central station, then to the conning tower. The conning tower changed steering control over from steam steering back to electric steering and finally transferred control back to the bridge.[3] This exercise demonstrated several of the many different means and locations from which to steer the ship. At the end of the day the *Texas* returned to her anchorage at Berth 47 and exercised the crew at fire quarters. The high state of training and readiness of the crew was evident by having the first stream of water at the scene of the "fire" in less than two minutes.

As the month of November progressed, rain, snow, and high winds became more common. When winds were particularly bad, the *Texas* would fire up her boilers, warm up her engines and prepare to get underway. Planes continued their daily flights as weather permitted, and the crew continued with various drills, exercises, and inspections.

Thursday, November 20 was Thanksgiving Day, and Chaplain W. W. Edel held divine services for the crew in the morning. It was a busy day for the cooks, who prepared a traditional Thanksgiving feast, including three hundred turkeys. The usual shore patrol and liberty parties went ashore, enjoying the limited pleasures of St. John's, Newfoundland. That afternoon the ammunition ship *Kilauea* came alongside and delivered a load of ammunition to the *Texas*. The crew brought aboard and carefully stowed ammunition for the 14-inch, 5-inch, 3-inch, and 1.1 inch anti-aircraft guns.

On Tuesday, November 25, 1941, there was a stir about the ship. At 10:15 A.M. an aviation gasoline lighter came alongside, and the *Texas* commenced taking on gasoline for her airplanes. Then at 12:20 P.M. the *Grackle* came alongside to starboard and transferred Admiral LeBreton's baggage to the *Texas*. Shortly thereafter, Rear Admiral D. M. LeBreton, Commander Battleships Atlantic Fleet, shifted his flag from *Arkansas* to *Texas*. At about 4:30 in the afternoon, the *Texas* got underway, proceeded out of the harbor, and formed up with the battleship *New York* and the destroyers *Sims* and *Morris*. *Sims* and *Morris* patrolled on anti-submarine stations ahead of *Texas*. The anti-aircraft guns and secondary battery were manned and ready as the *Texas* sailed out into the open ocean, headed for the United States.

On Friday, November 28, just before noon, the *Texas* anchored in Casco Bay, at Portland, Maine. Shortly after the ship's arrival, a twenty-six man shore patrol unit left the *Texas* for temporary duty in Portland, Maine. Later in the day the captain published the findings and sentences in the cases of three seamen tried by deck court martial for being absent over leave, or not returning to the ship when they were supposed to. All were found guilty and sentenced to ten days in the brig on bread and water, with a full ration of food every third day. Late that night a seaman was returned on board by the shore patrol charged with "Scandalous Conduct" and was placed in confinement by order of the commanding officer. During the next several days, sailors from the *Texas* enjoyed their liberty ashore, as young men will, little knowing their peacetime routine would soon be shattered by a vicious attack on the United States.

CHAPTER FIVE

"A Date That Will Live in Infamy"—The U.S. Enters World War II

As the month of December began, the battleship *Texas* was anchored in Berth 4 in Casco Bay at Portland, Maine. On Monday, the first day of December 1941, Capt. Lewis W. Comstock, who had assumed command of the ship on August 2, 1941, held mast for seventeen men and awarded punishments ranging from a warning to restriction to ship for ten days to deck court martial. The usual beach guard and shore patrol units went ashore for temporary duty, and the crew engaged in their shipboard routine and scheduled exercises for the next several days.

On Sunday, December 7, 1941, "a date which will live in infamy," the *Texas* remained anchored in her berth at Casco Bay. It was a quiet day on the ship, with little activity noted in the deck log. At 9:30 A.M. Rear Admiral Alexander Sharp, Commander Battleships Atlantic Fleet, hauled down his flag on the *Texas* and was relieved by Rear Admiral J.W. Wilcox. At 10:05 A.M. Rear Admiral Sharp hoisted his flag in *Arkansas* as Commander Battleship Division Five. The log of the *Texas* contains no mention of the attack on Pearl Harbor on December 7.[1]

Storekeeper Second Class Russell A. Morehouse was enjoying his liberty by taking in a movie in Portland, Maine. In the middle of the movie someone stopped the projector, and the manager of the theater announced that the Naval base at Pearl Harbor had been bombed. All service men were ordered to return to ship or station immediately.[2]

On Monday December 8, 1941, the ship's log contained this entry: "At 1400 received information that the Congress has declared the existence of a state of war between the United States and Japan." At 4:00 P.M. the crew darkened the ship and placed the secondary battery and searchlights in condition of readiness for possible attack by the enemy. In addition, the captain ordered picket boats to be stationed out in the bay to watch for submarines, frogmen, or saboteurs.

On Tuesday, December 9, there was a flurry of activity in the morning as various admirals and ship's captains conferred with one another aboard the *Texas*. At 1:00 P.M. the crew mustered at quarters, then the ship's company was paraded aft where Captain Comstock addressed the crew. He informed all hands of the existence of a state of hostilities between the United States and Japan, and as if to add emphasis to his message, his speech was interrupted by a report of the approach of hostile planes. The crew immediately went to general quarters and made preparations for getting underway. The report proved to be a false alarm, and, after two hours, the ship was secured from battle stations.

On Friday, December 12, 1941, the *Texas* got underway at 11:00 A.M. en route to Base Roger, Argentia Bay, Newfoundland, with the destroyers *Buck* and *Greer* acting as an anti-submarine screen. After passing through the anti-submarine net, the crew streamed out the ship's paravanes to protect her from mines. Once into the open sea, the captain sent the crew to General Quarters and fired twenty-four practice rounds from the 14-inch guns. The captain ordered the ship to commence zig-zag, to reduce the possibility of a successful torpedo attack. The ship's log for December 12 contained this Supplementary Note: "The United States this date declared war against Germany and Italy. Roger E. Nelson, Lt. Commander, U.S. Navy, Navigator."[3]

The *Texas* returned to Argentia Bay, Newfoundland, on December 14 and remained there over the Christmas holidays. The crew decided it would be a thoughtful gesture to invite the people of Conway,

Santa Claus handing out presents to the children of Conway, Newfoundland, on Christmas Day 1941.

Newfoundland, on board for Christmas, and the ship's chaplain, Commander W.W. Edel, made the arrangements. Conway was a small fishing village of about one hundred people, and the entire population of the town was the guest of the U.S.S. *Texas* for Christmas dinner. The crew treated the townspeople to their first American turkey dinner, after which the Americans played a movie for their visitors—the first motion picture for most of the villagers. The crew had decorated the ship by fitting out various quarters with fir branches, artificial fireplaces, Christmas trees, and nativity scenes. There were few ornaments on the ship or available in the area, so some of the more inventive sailors came up with a crude, if comical, substitute. They raided the medical department's prophylactic room and absconded with condoms. The sailors then inflated the condoms, painted them red and green, and placed them on the Christmas trees.[4]

The different compartments of the ship held a competition for the best decorated spaces, a competition won by the Marines. After dinner and the movie, Santa Claus (Chief Store Keeper William Hill) arrived in the captain's gig and was piped on board, attended by side boys. The crew assisted Santa Claus in giving gifts to all the children of the town. The sailors kept open the ship's geedunk stand, or soda fountain, and served free soda pop and ice cream to the children and townspeople. It was an enjoyable day for all hands, and the happiness of the crew was heightened by the arrival of 250 bags of mail, the first mail to arrive in three weeks.[5]

On the day after Christmas the mail boat delivered a letter to the ship.

Santa Clause   Newfoundland,
USS TEXAS   Ship Hr., P.B.,
                                           Dec 26th, 1941

Dear Santa Clause

I cannot tell you how thankful I was to receive all the presents which you gave me.

Well Santa it was the happiest Christmas I ever had. Do you know why?

Its because I spent it on-board the Texas and the most of all with you. How beautiful was the Ship with all the beauteful Christmas trees. And under one of the trees I saw the post office at Conway Cove where I live.

And even the movies were beautiful. Well dear Santa I am very thankful to you for all these things. There was a lot of excitement everything was beautiful. But you were the best of all you made us happy you made us merry and all of us wore a smile as you were giving us or presents.

Sailors from the U.S.S. Texas *salute Santa Claus as he boards the ship.*

Last night as I was Sleeping I had a beauteful dream one of my best dreams, it was about you. And when I awoke in the morning I was as happy as I was on board the Ship because you were on my mind.

Again thanking you for all you gifts & write soon

Your loving friend
William Tollett[6]

On the morning of Wednesday, January 7, 1942, the *Texas* fired up her boilers, warmed up her engines, and made all preparations for getting underway. Captain Comstock took the conn and, assisted by the navigator, got underway at 10:45 A.M. Passing through the anti-torpedo net entrance, the *Texas* moved out into the open sea and headed for New York. The destroyers *Livermore* and *Eberle* took station in anti-submarine screen. At 11:43 A.M. the ships commenced zig-zagging in order to frustrate any German U-boats that may have been in the area. Shortly thereafter, at 3:10 in the afternoon, a heavy snow squall with sleet set in, reducing visibility so badly that the lookouts could only see a little more than two hundred yards. The snow storm continued and increased in intensity, until by ten o'clock that night visibility was further reduced to a hundred yards.

The *Texas* entered New York harbor at 9:42 A.M. on Saturday, January 10, and soon anchored in the Naval Anchorage at Tomkinsville, New York. In New York, the *Texas* received 120 new sailors from the U.S. Naval Training Station at Newport, Rhode Island, as well as two new OS2U Kingfisher spotter planes. During the next few days the crew conducted routine repairs and brought aboard ammunition, fuels, and various supplies, including fifty thousand dollars from the Federal Reserve Bank of New York.

The *Texas* again prepared for getting left port on the morning of Thursday, January 15, 1942. Firing up all six boilers, the ship got underway in company with elements of Task Force 15 and stood out of the harbor. After passing through the anti-torpedo net gate the ship proceeded out through the swept channel to rendezvous with the remainder of Task Force 15, which consisted of the aircraft carrier *Wasp* as well as the heavy cruiser *Quincy*, troop ships *Munargo* and *Chateau Thierry*, Destroyer Division 16, and various patrol and minecraft. The destination of Task Force 15 was Base Cast, at Hvalfjordur, Iceland. The voyage from New York to Iceland took ten days because of constant snow squalls and rough seas. Heavy rain, fog, and hail added to the discomfort of the crew and lessened the visibility of the lookouts who strained their eyes to see submarines or the wake of torpedoes in the water. The task force finally arrived safely in Iceland on January 25, where the *Texas* remained for the next several weeks.[7]

On March 1, the *Texas*, in company with *Ericsson* and *Eberle*, left Hvalfjordur and headed for Norfolk, Virginia. The *Texas* soon ran into a storm that made the crossing a memorable, and a miserable, one for all hands. The first afternoon out of Iceland, winds of gale force and heavy waves damaged a motor whale boat so extensively it had to be thrown overboard. The following morning the crew jettisoned three other boats and the port paravane, all of which were damaged beyond repair by the high seas. The weather abated for a day then came back strong on March 7. On March 11 the hazardous crossing ended as the *Texas* and her escorts anchored in Narragansett Bay, Rhode Island. The ships sheltered there overnight, and arrived at the Norfolk Navy Yard on March 13, tying up at Pier 5 at 4:40 in the afternoon.[8]

On April 10, the *Texas* got underway at 4:30 in the morning and headed into the open sea, this time part of Task Force 38 headed toward the Panama Canal. Ships accompanying the *Texas* included *Brooklyn, McCauley, Formal Haut, Fuller Heywood, Neville, Bellatrix, Brostogi* and *Sommels Dyk*. A convoy from New York joined Task Force 38 at 8:00 A.M. The New York section included the *Barnett, Algorab, Betelgeuse, Almaak, Liggett, American Legion, Alhena, Elliot, Noordam*, and *Wanderer*. The transport ships escorted by the *Texas* carried the Fifth Marine Regiment and other elements of the 1st Marine Division, which had been activated on board the battleship only a year earlier. The crew of the *Texas* did not know it at the time, but the 1st Marine Division was on its way to Guadalcanal and the first American ground offensive of the war.

On April 18, the day Col. James Doolittle bombed Tokyo, the *Texas* safely delivered the Marines to the Canal Zone and briefly tied up at the pier at Cristobal. That evening the ship got underway for Norfolk, leaving the transport convoy to transit the canal and then make its way across the Pacific. Arriving back at the Norfolk Navy Yard on April 24, the *Texas* went into dry dock for a routine overhaul.[9]

After the *Texas* completed dry dock repairs, the Commander in Chief, Atlantic Fleet, ordered the creation of Task Force 34 with Captain Comstock in the *Texas* in command of the task force. The purpose of the task force was to escort a troop convoy to the vicinity of Freetown, Sierra Leone, on the west coast of Africa. Early in the morning of May 25, 1942, the *Texas*, accompanied by the destroyers

Dallas and *Ludlow*, departed Hampton Roads en route to Charleston, South Carolina. During the evening of May 26 the *Texas* arrived at Charleston, and Captain Comstock held a conference with the captains of the ships making up the troop convoy, the *Chateau Thierry*, *Mormacsun*, *Mariposa*, and *Santa Paula*. The escorts were the destroyers *Dallas*, *Cole*, *Bernadou*, and *Ludlow*. On the morning of May 28, Convoy AS-3 got underway from Charleston to Bermuda, where it anchored briefly at 8:15 A.M. on May 31. After refueling, the convoy again got underway at 3:00 P.M. At 10:40 that night the *Dallas* experienced an engine failure and returned to Bermuda, reducing the antisubmarine screen of the convoy. Shortly before the *Dallas* departed, the *Texas* received a warning of a submarine concentration along the path of the convoy. The next morning, at 5:35, the *Ludlow* reported a sound contact and made two attacks on the suspected submarines. While seeking out enemy submarines, the *Ludlow* discovered men in the water and rescued thirty-two survivors from a sunken British merchant ship. After effecting the rescue, the ships continued on their way with the destroyers screening the convoy and planes from the *Texas* scouting out the area during the day. At 5:55 A.M. on June 9, Convoy AS-3 arrived at the mid-ocean meeting point and met the British corvettes *Rock Rose* and *Violet*, which assumed the escort of the convoy. The *Texas*, *Ludlow*, *Bernadou*, and *Cole* headed back to Bermuda, refueled, and stood out for New York. While underway to New York, the *Texas* and her escorts stopped and inspected merchant ships with which the convoy came into contact. The *Texas* moored at Pier 51 at New York on June 19.[10]

The *Texas* left Tompkinsville, New York, on July 1, 1942, escorting convoy AT-17 sailing from New York to the United Kingdom via Halifax, Nova Scotia. The *Texas* was a part of Task Force 37, consisting additionally of the *Philadelphia*, *Trippe*, and Destroyer Squadron 13, escorting four U.S. Army transports, the *Monterrey*, *Barry*, *Argentina*, and *Siboney*. The convoy made its way across the Atlantic with the escorts making periodic sound contacts with real or imagined German U-boats and with the scout planes from the *Texas* and *Philadelphia* flying air patrol. Dense fog periodically plagued the convoy, making it very difficult to refuel the destroyers at sea but also reducing the necessity of zig-zagging. Making emergency turns to avoid suspected submarines almost daily while sailing in a thick fog caused many anxious moments during the voyage.

During the early morning hours of July 11, British Sunderland patrol planes flew over the convoy and provided air coverage. At 6:35 P.M. on July 11 the *Texas* sighted the coast of Ireland and continued on to the River Clyde in Scotland. At 7:35 in the morning of July 12, the *Texas* moored to a buoy off the port city of Greenock near Glasgow on the western coast of Scotland. Another convoy had been successfully delivered.[11]

The *Texas*, accompanied by the rest of Task Force 37 and the now-empty Army transports, headed back to the United States on July 18. British fighter planes provided an escort for the convoy as it made its way down the Firth of Clyde through the North Channel to the sea. After dawn on the 19th a heavy fog set in, canceling the much-desired air escort. The fog cleared on the following day, and the convoy set a speed of 15 knots. The *Philadelphia* and *Texas* periodically launched their scout planes to provide an anti-submarine patrol. The convoy made its way west, plagued by intermittently heavy fog and rain squalls. As the convoy approached New York, visibility decreased to zero and the *Texas* had to drop anchor and wait for a pilot before entering Tompkinsville anchorage. The next morning, July 28, *Texas* got underway for the Norfolk Navy Yard, escorted by a Navy blimp and a B-17. During the evening, the ship stood in to the Norfolk Navy Yard, Portsmouth, Virginia, and moored at Pier 4.[12]

The staff and personnel of Commander Battleships Atlantic Fleet, Rear Admiral Alexander Sharp, came aboard the *Texas* on August 10, and on August 19 the *Texas* moved to the Naval Operating Base at Hampton Roads, Virginia, to take on ammunition, fuel, and stores. Three days later, Rear Admiral Monroe Kelly relieved Rear Admiral Sharp as Commander Battleships, Atlantic Fleet. The time at Hampton Roads was well spent, with the crew preparing for impending activities. The crew held radar exercises with various ships and planes and honed their skills with the radio direction finder, main batteries, and anti-aircraft batteries. Damage control, general quarters, and air defense drills became more frequent, and the crew exercised with night general quarters drills and nighttime firing of the main batteries. Simulated attacks by bombing and torpedo planes leant a sense of realism and urgency to the air defense drills. Many in the crew felt that the combat debut of the *Texas* would soon be upon them. They were correct.

CHAPTER SIX

Guns Fired in Anger— The Invasion of North Africa

The first great offensive action by United States Army ground forces was the invasion of French North Africa in November 1942. Allied military planners first discussed the possibility of an invasion of French North Africa during the Arcadia Conference held in Washington during the week before Christmas in 1941. North Africa was a main topic of discussion for President Franklin D. Roosevelt, British Prime Minister Winston Churchill, and their military advisors, the Combined Chiefs of Staff.[1]

The Americans understood that the occupation of North Africa would prevent Axis subjugation of the area, help protect British lines of communication, and provide a base for further operations in the Mediterranean and southern Europe. But the Americans preferred an early strike in Western Europe.[2]

The British, while acknowledging that Western Europe would eventually have to be invaded, were hesitant to launch an early attack.[3] The memory of catastrophic land campaigns in World War I against Germany was indelible in the British military mind. They preferred not to challenge the German Army in Europe until it had been

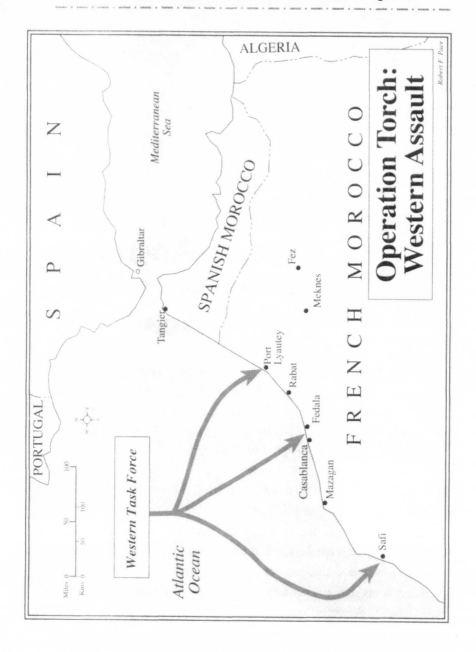

worn down by attrition. The British preferred a strategy of peripheral action or encirclement rather than direct confrontation.

President Roosevelt, alone among the Americans, was an early advocate of a North African campaign. He believed it afforded American forces an early opportunity to confront German forces, essential to American morale, while an all-out invasion of Europe would require a much larger build-up and consequently much more time for preparation.[4]

In June 1942, the British Eighth Army was badly mauled by German Field Marshall Erwin Rommel's Afrika Korps in Libya. During the same month, the Afrika Korps captured the British fortress of Tobruk in eastern Libya near the Egyptian border. The German advance through Egypt toward the Suez Canal, Britain's lifeline from the Mediterranean to her Indian Empire, made it impossible for Britain to contemplate an invasion of Europe in 1942 and probably 1943.[5]

Gen. George C. Marshall, chief of staff of the United States Army, and Admiral Ernest J. King, chief of naval operations of the United States Navy, were both opposed to the invasion of North Africa. They viewed such an operation as a diversion from the main allied objective of defeating the German Army and liberating Europe. The two American military leaders went so far as to suggest if Britain had no desire to invade Europe, America would turn its back on Europe and turn the full might of American armed forces against Japan.[6]

President Roosevelt refused to consider any action that appeared to abandon the British, however, and he directed General Marshall and Admiral King to come to an agreement with the British concerning strategic aims. General Marshall and Admiral King therefore reluctantly agreed to an American-British invasion of North Africa.[7]

The decision to invade French Morocco and Algeria was ultimately both political and military. The invasion would show the American public and the world that the United States was definitely in the war and taking aggressive action against Germany and Italy. A successful campaign would deny Germany the use of northwest Africa as a submarine and aircraft base. Ejection of German and Italian forces from North Africa would ensure that Allied convoys could use the Mediterranean to reach the British possessions of Egypt, Malta, and India. And finally, Allied planners hoped the offensive against German troops in North Africa would aid beleaguered Russia.

After Hitler had defeated France and ejected the British Army from the European continent, he ignored his non-aggression pact with Joseph Stalin and turned Germany's full force and fury upon the Soviet Union. By the middle of 1942, Soviet forces were hard-pressed by the German Army. The American and British commanders realized that some effort had to be made to relieve the pressure on the Soviet Army, or the Soviet Union might be defeated or ask Hitler for peace terms before the eventual liberation of Europe by Allied forces. It was imperative to take some immediate action against the German Army. Allied military planners believed action against the German Army in North Africa would draw German military resources away from Russia, giving the Red Army a much-needed respite.[8]

After the tentative agreement for a joint British and American invasion of French North Africa had been reached, the planning began. American and British staff officers conferred in numerous meetings on both sides of the Atlantic, working out the details of the invasion. They had to confront and find solutions for great problems of distance, logistics, and secrecy. The British and American staffs worked tirelessly to develop an acceptable plan with a good chance for success.

The Combined Chiefs of Staff decided that the attacks should occur in three places: Casablanca on the Atlantic coast of French Morocco, and at both Oran and Algiers on the Mediterranean coast of Algeria.[9] The Allied forces assigned to Operation Torch were therefore divided into three major parts, Western, Center, and Eastern.

The Western Naval Task Force, also known as Task Force 34, was under the command of Rear Admiral H. Kent Hewitt. This task force embarked the Western Task Force United States Army under the command of Maj. Gen. George S. Patton. General Patton's forces were responsible for the capture of Casablanca and adjacent areas.

The Center Naval Task Force was under the command of Commodore Thomas Troubridge, Royal Navy. This task force embarked the Center Task Force United States Army under Maj. Gen. Lloyd R. Fredendall and had Oran as its objective.

The Eastern Naval Task Force, under Rear Admiral Sir H.M. Burrough, Royal Navy, carried the Eastern Assault Force. Maj. Gen. Charles W. Ryder, commander of the Eastern Assault Force, was to capture Algiers. The overall commander of the North African invasion was Maj. Gen. Dwight D. Eisenhower, U.S. Army.[10]

The mission of the Western Task Force was to secure the port at Casablanca and the airfields in the area. American military planners believed that Casablanca was too heavily defended to take by direct assault, so they planned for the ground forces to capture it from the rear. The main infantry force would land at Fedala, only eighteen miles north of Casablanca, while American tanks would land at the port of Safi, 140 miles south of Casablanca. Air superiority was necessary for the successful completion of the mission, and that required an airfield from which U.S. Army aircraft could operate. The best airfield in the area was at Port Lyautey, seventy-eight miles north of Casablanca.[11] The 60th Infantry Regiment of the U.S. Army's Ninth Infantry Division, commanded by Brig. Gen. Lucian Truscott, drew the mission of capturing Port Lyautey itself, the site of the only concrete, all-weather landing strip in North Africa. The battleship *Texas,* the aging veteran of the First World War, was ordered to provide gunfire support for the men of the 60th Infantry.

To support the ground phase of the operation, the Western Naval Task Force was divided into four separate groups. These were the Covering Group, the Northern Attack Group, the Center Attack Group, and the Southern Attack Group. In command of the Northern Attack Group, designated Task Force 34.3, would be Rear Admiral Monroe Kelly, sailing aboard the *Texas.* Besides the *Texas,* other ships in the Northern Attack Group included the light cruiser *Savannah,* auxiliary aircraft carriers *Sangamon* and *Chenango,* nine destroyers, and numerous transports, cargo ship, and other auxiliaries.

In the weeks leading up to the departure of Task Group 34.3, the *Texas* experienced several changes in command. The skipper of the *Texas*, Capt. L.W. Comstock, suffered a mild heart attack and was transferred to the Naval Hospital at Portsmouth, Virginia. The ship's executive officer, Commander W.E. Hennigar, assumed temporary command of the vessel. He continued preparations for the coming conflict, including general quarters exercises, simulated battle problems, and underway fueling exercises. While the *Texas* was under the command of Commander Hennigar, Rear Admiral Monroe Kelly conducted the annual military inspection and damage control practice for the battleship. Capt. Lawrence Wild reported on board the *Texas* for duty as the new commanding officer on October 3, and Commander Hennigar reverted to his previous position as executive officer. Captain Wild's tenure was short-lived, however, as on October 14 he was transferred to Naval Hospital, Portsmouth, Virginia, suffering from war neurosis. Commander Hennigar once again assumed command of the ship. Preparations for battle continued with shore bombardment and anti-aircraft exercises, and on October 17, Capt. Roy Pfaff reported aboard and assumed command of the *Texas*.[12] Pfaff would lead the crew and the ship for the next seventeen months.

The armada that was to make up the invasion force gathered in various ports on the eastern seacoast of the United States. The fleet, with more than one hundred ships, was considered too large to sail from a single port without attracting unwanted attention, so the plan called for the vessels to depart from various bases in smaller groups and rendezvous at sea.

The battleship *Texas* weighed anchor at 8:00 A.M. on October 23 and moved down the channel from Hampton Roads, Virginia. It formed up with the rest of the convoy and headed for the open sea.[13] The days that followed were anxious ones, as there was bright moonlight from sunset to sunrise, ideal conditions for a submarine attack. On October 24, one of the screening destroyers made underwater sound contact, and the convoy made an emergency turn of 45 degrees to port to avoid a possible enemy submarine. Captain Pfaff ordered two of the spotter planes of the *Texas* aloft as an anti-submarine patrol.[14] The crew of the *Texas* sighted the Covering Force and the remainder of the invasion convoy on October 26, and on the following day the *Texas* took her position in the main convoy, Task Force 34.[15]

The fleet continued zigzagging its way eastward, refueling from the oil transports as necessary, and responding to real or imagined sound contacts reported by the destroyer screen. On a few occasions the destroyers dropped patterns of depth charges on the location of sound contacts, but no submarines were actually sighted. The Vought OS2U Kingfisher spotter planes of the *Texas* relinquished their anti-submarine patrol duties to the aircraft of the escort carriers, and general quarters and anti-aircraft exercises continued. The skies became more overcast, and rainsqualls occurred frequently.[16]

The fleet parted company on November 7 as the Southern Attack Group turned south toward its assigned target. The Northern and Center Attack Groups continued steaming eastward. At 3:00 P.M. these two groups pulled apart, the Center Attack Group heading for Fedhala and Casablanca, while the Northern Attack Group, under the command of Rear Admiral Monroe Kelly in the *Texas*, continued on toward Mehedia on the northwest coast of French Morocco. The *Texas* led the Northern Attack Group to its assigned position, arriving there just before midnight.[17]

As the *Texas* drew near the Moroccan coast, Rear Admiral Kelly sent the following message to Brigadier General Truscott: "On the eve of our joint operation in the Northern Attack Area I wish to assure you of the Navy's cooperation in every respect with you and your troops. The Navy's duty is to protect the transports, operate landing boats and support the Army with gun fire upon your landing in Morocco." He further assured the general, "This we shall do to the utmost. It will be a historical operation. If you meet with resistance," he concluded, "give them hell."

Admiral Kelly also had an encouraging message for his own men: "We are about to embark upon a most difficult and historical task— the opening of a second front in Africa." He reminded the men that the "people back home and the entire United Nations will watch us with consuming interest. Don't let them down." He then appealed to history and tradition to inspire the sailors. He wrote: "To successfully carry out our task we must live up to the glorious past of the Navy which will require the utmost from all hands and duty beyond the usual call. This is our opportunity to strike a blow for America and our allies. Let us be ready to give the enemy hell whenever and wherever we meet him."[18]

The army did not request a pre-landing bombardment for two reasons. American leaders hoped that the French forces in Morocco would not resist the U.S. invasion, in which case a bombardment would be unnecessary. If the French did decide to resist, the Americans wanted the landing to be a surprise. Additionally, General Truscott questioned the accuracy and benefit of naval gunfire. The general hoped and believed that his troops could capture their objectives before the French defenders could mount an effective resistance. He was sadly mistaken.[19]

H-hour, the time for the troops to hit the beach, had been set for 4:00 A.M. on November 8, but getting the Army troops off the transports and into the landing craft took longer than expected. In the predawn darkness, the heavily burdened soldiers of the 60th Infantry Regiment clambered over the sides of the three transports, *Susan B. Anthony, George Clymer,* and *Henry T. Allen,* and struggled down cargo nets into the awaiting landing boats. The boats shoved off, formed up, and made their way to the landing beaches through heavy surf with waves up to six feet high. The first troops began landing at about 5:30 in the morning, an hour and a half after schedule, and quickly established a small beachhead while the *Texas* maintained a position in her fire support area about six miles off shore.[20] The leaders of the French Army in North Africa, confused as to who were their friends and who were their enemies, decided to align themselves with their German conquerors. The French Army fired on the American troops and the battle began.

On two occasions during those anxious hours of the morning of November 8, the crew of the *Texas* fired on American airplanes that strayed too close to the battleship. At 8:05 a group of four airplanes came up from astern the *Texas* on the port quarter. The crew manning the aft anti-aircraft batteries, involved in their first action, opened fire on the trailing airplane, then all the anti-aircraft guns on the port side followed suit. The aircraft quickly climbed into the low-lying clouds, and none of the planes were hit. The inexperienced and somewhat jittery anti-aircraft gun crews fired 640 rounds of twenty-millimeter ammunition and 178 rounds of 1.1-inch ammunition at the American planes without effect.[21]

A second incident occurred at 9:22 when American airplanes dropped out of the cloud cover directly over the stern of the ship. The guns opened up again, and the planes quickly climbed into the clouds, evading the fire. The crew fired 470 rounds of twenty-millimeter and 118 rounds of 1.1-inch ammunition at the planes, apparently without hitting any of them.[22] Later in the war the aim of the gunners improved.

Early that afternoon, Army Shore Fire Control Party Number One called for naval gunfire on the munitions dump near Port Lyautey. For the first time since the *Texas* was commissioned in 1914, the twenty-seven year old warship fired her main battery at an enemy target. The gun crews of turrets two and four trained the turrets out to starboard and pointed their barrels into the air. At 1:43 P.M. the 14-inch rifles roared, and yellow flame and clouds of brown smoke erupted from the barrels as the *Texas* opened fire at 16,500 yards, or just over eight miles. The shore fire control party, as well as Lieutenant Turner in his OS2U-3 Kingfisher spotter plane of the *Texas*, observed the impact of the shells. After the *Texas* fired fifty-nine rounds of 14-inch ammunition, the shore fire control party called and said that no more fire was needed, so the bombardment was stopped at 2:03 P.M., just twenty minutes after the guns started firing. The pilot of the spotter plane reported that about twenty percent of the 14-inch shells hit in the target area that was on a reverse slope or back side of a hill, and he counted ten definite craters in the target area. The shelling destroyed one magazine and damaged two other buildings, including the commandant's quarters. Four duds landed in the prison grounds adjacent to the ammunition dump. As many as one third of the 14-inch rounds failed to explode.[23]

At about sunset, Lieutenant Turner landed his Kingfisher next to the *Texas* for recovery and tore off a wing-tip float. The Kingfisher capsized, but Turner and Aviation Radioman First Class Vaughan, the back-seat man, escaped uninjured and were rescued from the sea by the minesweeper *Raven*, which then sank the overturned airplane with gunfire. French gunners had been firing at the airplane, and it may have been struck by anti-aircraft fire that caused the accident.[24]

On the morning of November 10, Army observers ashore noticed enemy trucks carrying troops on the road toward Port Lyautey from Meknes and called for the *Texas* to fire on the road. The 14-inch gunners opened fire from 17,000 yards with turrets two and four and fired 150 rounds of 14-inch shells and six rounds of 5-inch shells. The spotter plane from the *Texas* reported that traffic had halted on the road, and the fire was stopped. Later in the morning the *Texas* spotter plane pilot reported that traffic on the road was moving again, so the mighty battleship resumed firing. The massive 14-inch shells scored direct hits on the road and its shoulders and destroyed many vehicles. After the gunners fired sixty-four rounds of 14-inch ammunition, the pilot of the spotter plane reported that the road was impassible and all traffic had once again halted. Captain Pfaff then gave the order to cease fire. No traffic moved on the road for the remainder of the day.[25]

During the bombardment of the 10th, two OS2U-3 Kingfisher spotter planes from the *Texas* flew reconnaissance. Ensign L.D. Hollingsworth, Jr., one of the pilots, observed a motorcycle with a sidecar speeding away from Port Lyautey. Hollingsworth thought the sidecar might contain a high-ranking officer, so he pursued the motorcycle. Dropping down to less than one hundred feet, he strafed it with his nose-mounted thirty-caliber machinegun, causing the motorcycle and sidecar to crash into a ditch. Then Hollingsworth turned his attention to several enemy trucks on the road, some of them towing artillery pieces. He dove on the trucks firing his

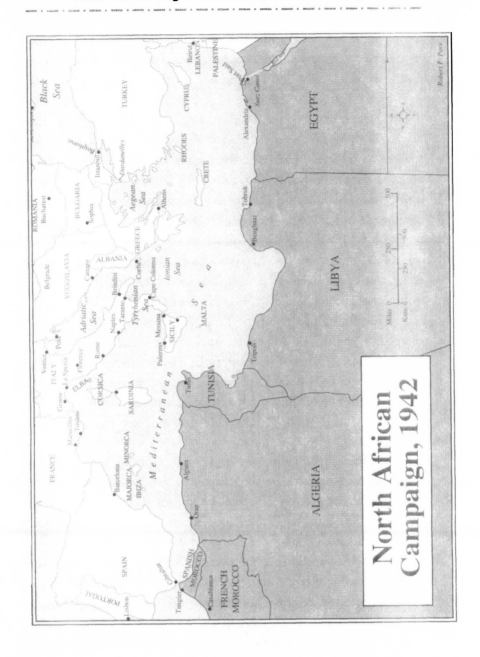

North African Campaign, 1942

Robert F. Post

machinegun, while his radio operator in the back seat also opened fire. The rear cockpit of the Kingfisher was equipped with a flexible machinegun, mounted on a tilting and rotating seat, which could be fired to the rear or to the side of the airplane. The pilot and radio operator expended all their ammunition, hitting four or five of the trucks. With his machineguns empty, Hollingsworth then pulled out his Colt forty-five caliber automatic pistol and, leaning out of the cockpit, continued his strafing runs until he had fired all eighteen rounds from his sidearm. During the attacks, machinegun fire from the ground struck Hollingsworth's Kingfisher in the left wing, but the bullet holes caused only slight damage to the airplane.[26]

At 2:35 that afternoon, Army troops ashore reported that French tanks and trucks were advancing northward toward Port Lyautey from Rabat and requested an air attack on the road. Lt. W.R. Turner was in the air, flying one of the Kingfishers from the *Texas*, and he charged to the attack. When he reached the scene of the action, Turner joined a Curtis SOC spotter plane from another ship as well as a Grumman F4F-4 Wildcat fighter and a Grumman TBF Avenger bomber from one of the aircraft carriers. Lieutenant Turner and the composite attack group strafed the column, setting one truck ablaze.[27]

When the call for help came in, Lt. L.R. Chesley, Jr., was in the cockpit of his Kingfisher on the catapult of the *Texas* with a Mark II depth charge mounted on the plane's bomb rack. The aviation crew set the fuse of the depth charge to explode instantaneously on impact, and when the catapult's gunpowder charge fired, Chesley's Kingfisher shot into the air. He joined the action over the Rabat road and glided over the tank column, releasing his depth charge at an altitude of one thousand feet. In spite of heavy anti-aircraft fire from machineguns and anti-aircraft artillery, Chelsey scored a direct hit on one tank with the depth charge, destroying it. The explosion overturned two other tanks. Chesley then joined the other planes in strafing attacks, dropping as low as fifty feet above the ground. In addition to destroying the three tanks, the American planes blew up one truck and seriously damaged and immobilized three others.[28]

A number of reporters had joined the ships of the fleet prior to its leaving the United States. One young United Press reporter observed the naval shelling of North Africa from the bridge of the *Texas* and was greatly impressed by the fire, smoke, and searing heat from the 14-inch guns. After the battle, he was the first reporter to file a story covering the invasion, garnering a measure of fame for himself and the United Press. The reporter, Walter Cronkite, continued as a war correspondent for the rest of the long conflict but witnessed his first action as an observer on the *Texas*.

During the invasion of North Africa, the battleship *Texas* became a floating broadcasting station. Army communications technicians installed special radio equipment on board the ship under the control of officers from the Office of War Information. Shortly after H-hour on November 8, the French-speaking American news commentator Andre Baruch and others broadcast appeals to the French soldiers in North Africa to stop fighting the Americans. He broadcast proclamations of President Roosevelt and General Eisenhower, in French, reminding the Frenchmen of the long friendship between the two countries. He also played recordings of music including the national anthems of the United States and France and "God Bless America" and "Colonel Bogey March."[29] Unfortunately the appeals went unheeded or unheard, and the French troops continued fighting until they were instructed to lay down their arms by Admiral Darlan, the commander in chief of the French forces in North Africa, on November 10. All French resistance ceased on November 11.[30]

After the conclusion of the fighting a number of U.S. Army soldiers and officers came aboard the *Texas*. As the Army officers conversed with the battleship's captain and other officers, a sergeant ran up to turret three, climbed the ladder to the top of the turret and walked out onto one of the 14-inch barrels. He sat down on the barrel, straddling it like a horse, and leaned forward, hugging and kissing the gun. Buglemaster Will John Eddleman asked the sergeant what was the matter with him. The sergeant replied that the guns had saved the lives of many of the American soldiers. He went on to relate that the Army troops had passed through Port Lyautey with ease, but when they got out into the desert they were attacked by tanks. As the soldiers had no anti-tank weapons, they had to retreat all the way back to the shoreline. Then the *Texas* opened up with her 14-inch guns and destroyed the tanks, hurling some of them up into the air. The soldiers regrouped, secured the town, and the battle was won. Upon hearing the sergeant's report, the men of the *Texas* swelled with justifiable pride.[31]

During the fighting, the French had sunk a number of ships in the river that led from the sea to Port Lyautey. Lieutenant Blackburn, an engineering officer, formed a team of *Texas* sailors to salvage the scuttled vessels. The salvage team first went to work on the Dutch freighter *Export* and spent the night salvaging what they could. During the night, the tide went out and the ship lay over on her side. Dishes, chairs, and other gear went crashing and rattling through the ship, startling the anxious *Texas* sailors who for a few tense moments thought they were under attack. The next day the salvage crew raised the ship, which was subsequently used to transfer stores from transports to Port Lyautey.[32]

The *Texas* salvage team next went to work on the Swedish steamer *Nyhorn*, and had salvage operations well underway when they received the distressing news on November 15 that the *Texas* had sailed for the United States. The salvage crew caught a ride on a minesweeper to Casablanca, then boarded the U.S.S. *Livermore*, also bound for the states. After two days sailing, on November 19 the *Livermore* caught up with the *Texas*, and the salvage team transferred over to their home ship by a breeches buoy, a canvas seat pulled on a rope between the two vessels. Shortly after the four officers and thirty-five enlisted men from the *Texas* boarded their ship, the breast lines joining the two ships broke in the heavy seas.[33]

The *Texas* dropped anchor once again at Hampton Roads, Virginia, on November 27, and her victorious crewmen enjoyed their well-earned liberty ashore. The aging battleship and her crew would participate in other invasions: Normandy, Southern France, Iwo Jima, and Okinawa. This invasion of French Morocco, however, had been a learning experience, a time of acquiring the skills and confidence necessary for success. Operation Torch had been a great victory, the first step on the long road to liberation for North Africa and Europe. The veteran battleship *Texas* and her gallant crew had been an integral part in the first action that led to ultimate victory for the Allied cause.

CHAPTER SEVEN

Operation Overlord—
The Invasion of France

After the excitement of the Invasion of North Africa, the crew of the *Texas* settled into a less demanding, though still important and dangerous, role as convoy escort. Based primarily in New York, the *Texas* made numerous transatlantic voyages to Casablanca, Gibraltar, Scotland, and Northern Ireland, always safely delivering ships full of equipment, supplies, and soldiers. In June 1943, workers at the Boston Navy Yard installed forty 40-millimeter anti-aircraft guns in ten quadruple mounts to replace the inadequate and obsolete 1.1-inch guns.

During the first few months of 1944 the convoy escort routine continued, and January found the *Texas* escorting Convoy UT-6 from America to Britain across the often stormy North Atlantic seas. During the morning of January 3, the crew discovered that the anti-submarine blister on the port side had cracked and had peeled back. Three days later the blister sheared completely off from frame 22 to frame 26, or a distance of sixteen feet. As soon as the *Texas* delivered the convoy safely to its destination, the aging battlewagon made its way to Tail O' The Bank, in the River Clyde Estuary, on the western coast of Scotland, anchoring there on January 7, 1944. Once the Scottish yard workers affected temporary repairs to the blister, the *Texas* made its way back home, escorting Convoy TU-6 from British waters to the east coast of the U.S.[1]

Quad-40 anti-aircraft guns.

The *Texas* entered dry dock in the Boston Navy Yard on January 23, for a general overhaul, including repair of the damaged blister and other leaking blisters and the cleaning and painting of the ship's bottom. The ship exited dry dock on February 4, but Boston Navy Yard workers continued repairs and upgrades to the old dreadnought until February 24. During this time, all the turret shell hoists were modified for the new type of 14-inch shells, and all the old type ammunition was turned in and replaced with newer armor-piercing and high-capacity 14-inch shells. Additionally, the SG surface search radar was relocated to the fore top, and high frequency direction finding equipment was installed. Finally, the Combat Information Center, or CIC, was modernized and brought up to the latest standards of equipment and organization.

The *Texas* once again headed out to open sea on February 25, 1944, for post-repair trials, and then sailed north for Casco Bay, Maine, where she anchored on February 27. During the first few weeks of March, the crew exercised regularly in damage control and

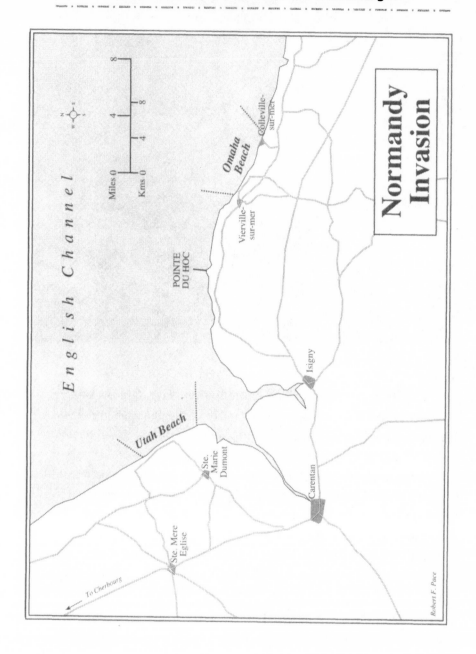

anti-aircraft gunnery with the 20-millimeter, 40-millimeter, and 3-inch guns. The crews of the 5-inch broadside guns also had a work-out, as did the sailors operating the ship's radar.[2]

A notable interruption in the ship's routine occurred on Friday, March 10, 1944, at 2:00 in the afternoon. Capt. Charles A. Baker relieved Capt. Roy Pfaff as the commanding officer of the U.S.S. *Texas*. After the arrival of Captain Baker the training continued, and on March 31 the *Texas* sailed from Casco Bay to New York. Upon arrival, Rear Admiral Carleton F. Bryant, commander of Battleship Division 5, boarded the *Texas* and hoisted his two-star flag above its mast. Battleship Division 5 consisted of the *Texas, Nevada, Arkansas,* and *New York*.[3]

On April 6, the *Texas* once again got underway and sailed down the North River to the open sea where the ship met up with elements of Convoy UT-11 on its way to England. During the trip across the North Atlantic, escorting destroyers dropped depth charges on suspected submarines several times, and the entire convoy had to change course once to avoid icebergs. As the convoy reached the approaches to Scotland, the ships proceeded independently to their various assigned ports, and the *Texas* continued on to the Tail O'Bank, in the Clyde Estuary in Scotland, dropping anchor there at 3:32 in the morning of April 16.[4]

After ten days of rest, occasional liberty, and routine maintenance, the crew of the *Texas* began an intense period of training with special emphasis on shore bombardment. Sometimes the 14-inch gun crews practiced with airplane spotters and at other times with Shore Fire Control Parties from the *Texas* that went ashore in motor whale boats. The exercises continued almost daily, as the crew improved their methods of fire control and communications with spotters ashore. Gunnery exercises were also held at night, using radar to aim the big 14-inch rifles. The *Nevada* and *Arkansas* joined with the *Texas* in the gunnery drills, and the three old dreadnoughts conducted communications drills between ships and with air spotting by both British and U.S. aircraft observers, as well as with Naval Shore Fire Control Parties. It was obvious to all the crew that momentous times were ahead, and training with British aircraft and ships indicated a joint effort in European waters. It did not take great imagination to suspect that the intensive training was for the invasion of German-occupied France.[5]

The staff officers planning the invasion realized very early that spotting the naval gunfire from ship-based spotter planes would be problematic. The waters near the invasion beaches would be crowded with numerous sea craft, and the spotter planes would have difficulty landing near their assigned ships. Additionally, enemy anti-aircraft fire and enemy airplanes could make things decidedly dangerous for the Navy's unarmored and lightly armed Voight OS2U Kingfisher observations planes. So someone came up with the idea of putting the Kingfishers ashore in England and using British Supermarine Spitfire airplanes flying from England as spotter planes for the U.S. battleships and heavy cruisers. Seventeen pilots from the battleships *Texas*, *Nevada*, and *Arkansas*, as well as the cruisers *Quincy*, *Augusta*, and *Tuscaloosa* formed a special squadron, VCS-7, to provide aerial observation for the big guns during the invasion of France. Observation Squadron 5, or VO5 (the air crew of the *Texas*), transferred on May 1 to a Royal Air Force Base at Lee-on-Solent, Hampshire, England, for training in fighter observation.

The new squadron formed in England and the pilots began an intensive training period which lasted from May 8 until May 28, during which the men learned how to fly the Spitfire fighter. The Spitfire was a much more powerful airplane than the Kingfisher, and the pilots learned how to dogfight with the aircraft, as well as how to spot naval gunfire with the much faster Spitfire. The program was quite successful, with only one plane and pilot lost in 191 combat sorties between June 6 and June 26 when the squadron was disbanded.[6]

During the first three weeks of May, the crew of the *Texas*, *Nevada*, *Arkansas*, and various British ships continually engaged in gunnery and damage control training in preparation for future operations. Communications experts from the U.S. Army installed special communications equipment during this period, also. The new radios included transmitters and receivers for communicating with Army aircraft and Army Shore Fire Control Parties, as well as transmitters to jam German radars and a special transmitter to jam German radio guided missiles. On May 8 the *Texas* reported for duty in Task Group 129.2, for special training in the Belfast area. Ships assigned to the task group and participating in the exercises were the *Texas*, *Arkansas*, His Majesty's Ship (HMS) *Glasgow*, and the French cruisers *Georges Leygues* and *Montcalm*. Training during the next several days placed special emphasis on anti-aircraft gunnery.[7]

While temporarily stationed at Belfast, Ireland, the crew of the *Texas* enjoyed weekends at Belfast Lough and in the green Irish countryside nearby. On Friday, May 19, 1944, Gen. Dwight David Eisenhower, Supreme Commander of the Allied Expeditionary Force, accompanied by the Naval Commander of the Western Task Force, Rear Admiral Allan G. Kirk, visited the *Texas* at Belfast. The crew was assembled on deck aft to hear the remarks on an overcast, rainy day. As General Eisenhower stepped up to the microphone, he noticed that none of the men were wearing coats or jackets. Before beginning his speech, General Eisenhower removed his raincoat so he would be exposed to the elements, as were the men. He immediately had the loyalty and respect of every man there.[8] The speech of General Eisenhower made a vivid impression on the officers and men of the *Texas*:

> No man could be more honored than I in the opportunity to come out here this morning and on this ship, which by coincidence is named after the state of my birth, to welcome here into the great Allied team that has been operating in the European theatre for the past 18 months, the officers and men of the ships that have come to bear their part in the beginning of the real attack on Axis Europe.
>
> I assure you that standing here this morning, there is not only the pride of an American in a great institution, one of which we are so proud at home, but I think I have the feeling that here in these mighty ships and in their crews, there is with me once and for all in this thing, the might and tradition of the United States Navy, coupled up with similar forces of His Majesty's Navy, and that there is a support that has come to me that makes me feel better than I have in the 18 long months. I am truly thrilled.

The text books that most of your senior officers have followed as they have gone through the services, say that the high commander should go down and inspect the troops in order to inspire them and in order to impress his personality upon them. In my case, I must be a throwback, or monkey, or something is wrong, because I always carry back to my own desk a thrill and inspiration that comes only when I get to see the fighting men. Because this is one thing I would like all of you to remember. There are limitations in war upon what the High Command can do. Admiral Kirk has given me some credit for getting these United States Ships here. Well, I certainly argued and cursed enough about it. But after all, that is just getting them over. The High Command can get you the supplies, can make sure of your preparations, it can make sure that your air coverage is present because in the next battle we are going into, we are going in with the greatest air coverage that has ever accompanied you and your forces in history. They provide for taking care of you when wounded, they see that you are disposed properly, that your guns are turned on the right targets, *but, my God men, you do the fighting.* No General or any other person in high capacity really fires the shots that knock out the enemy batteries and sinks the ships. *You are the people who do it. You are the men handling the guns and turrets, the men handling the firing of the weapons, torpedoes, Bofors, everything. You are the men who are winning the war.* You have come to do it, and all we can do is see that everything is made ready, and then you, with your American courage, your American indomitable will to win, have got to be at your best. *KNOCK THAT DAMNED HITLER OUT OF THE WAR.* Yours is the job and you are the men that the United States is going to be proud of.

God bless you all and good luck go with every one of you. Let me tell you the feeling that you are in there pitching with us is a great one for me as I contemplate the great day.[9]

Gen. Dwight D. Eisenhower tours the U.S.S. Texas.

Following the speech, General Eisenhower made an informal tour of the ship, accompanied by Rear Admiral Kirk, Rear Admiral Bryant, Captain Baker, and other American and British officers.[15]

The ships of Task Group 129.2 conducted a night battle problem on May 25, simulating a night bombardment in support of an infantry assault, during which the crew remained at General Quarters for ten hours. At the conclusion of the exercise on May 26, all the ships returned to their anchorages in Belfast, and for the next five days the crew intermixed liberty and recreation ashore with stripping the ship for battle. Finally, on May 31, Captain Baker received orders to seal the ship from all contacts ashore and to open all bags and envelopes containing the orders for Operation Neptune.[11] That evening, Captain Baker addressed the crew over the ship's broadcasting system and announced that the vessel had been "sealed" as of 8 o'clock that morning. He explained: "That means that the great events for which all of you have been working and preparing will shortly be launched. It also means that every possible effort must be made to prevent any leakage whatever of information in coming

Chaplain LeGrande Moody on the loudspeaker the night before D-Day.

operations, by whatever means—mail, personal contact, or signals." He continued by stating that he considered the men "now at battle efficiency and the time has come to polish up our weapons. From now until D-day only such drills as are necessary to maintain your present state will be conducted. But remember," he warned, "the enemy we are going up against will tax our readiness to the utmost. WE HAVE GOT TO BE GOOD."[12]

During the next two days the senior officers studied the plans for Operations Neptune, the naval portion of Operation Overlord—the Invasion of France. After becoming familiar with the plans, the officers then briefed all the ship's personnel on the upcoming battle. On June 3 at about 2:00 A.M., the *Texas*, followed by the other ships of the bombardment group of the Western Task Force, got underway from Belfast and began sailing south, to go around the southwestern tip of England known as Land's End, toward Normandy, France. The men of the aging battleship knew that an incredible battle lay before them, as the invasion of occupied Europe was scheduled for 6:30 in the morning on Monday, June 5, 1944.

All day Saturday, June 3 the *Texas* sailed through the Irish Sea, and the sailors saw more and more ships, all moving toward the English Channel. The weather was bad, the sea was stormy and rough, and many of the *Texas* sailors wondered if the small landing craft would be able to operate in such heaving seas. At about 7:00 in the morning of Sunday, June 4, Captain Baker received a message that "D-Day" had been postponed for twenty-four hours. The battlewagon reversed course for twelve hours, then turned about and reversed again, burning up the twenty-four hours and putting the ship back in its proper place at the proper time.

By mid-afternoon on Monday, June 5 the *Texas* was in the English Channel, and the other ships of the Omaha Beach bombardment group formed up in the waters off Plymouth, England, and steamed toward France. The men on deck could see hundreds of ships of every size in every direction. Barrage balloons floated over the landing ships and transports, and far overhead was a constant umbrella of Allied planes. At about 10:50 P.M. during the night of June 5, general quarters sounded on the *Texas*, and the crew went to their battle stations. Shortly thereafter the old dreadnought entered a massive German minefield, only recently cleared by U.S. and British minesweepers. Once in the swept lanes, the *Texas* had to dodge several groups of landing craft that were struggling in the heavy seas and strong tides. A Landing Craft, Medium, or LCM, apparently unable to overcome the strong cross-current, headed right for the comparatively gigantic battleship. Chaplain LeGrande Moody was on the bridge using the ship's loudspeaker system to give a play-by-play description of the scene and unfolding events for the benefit of the crew at their battle stations deep within the interior of the *Texas*. "Stand by for a ram on the port bow," he announced, just before the LCM struck the port bow of the battleship. Making the collision announcement was almost comical, for the collision was like a bug hitting the windshield of a car. No one on the

Officers from the Texas *examine German installations damaged by their ship's gunfire on D-Day.*

Texas even felt the collision, but it was lucky for the LCM that it was only a glancing blow. The LCM, loaded with assault troops, backed up and continued on its way with no apparent damage. At last, by 5:30 on the morning of June 6, the *Texas* was in her assigned position 12,000 yards, or just under seven miles, from the French shoreline, with the ship's port broadside to the beach.[13]

The bridge of the *Texas* was crowded. Capt. Charles A. Baker was there, along with his Marine orderly. The helmsman, several phone talkers, a radar operator, a bugler, and a quartermaster taking notes for the captain's log filled most of the available space in the crowded navigation bridge. Everyone there knew that the first troops would storm ashore to their unknown fate at 6:30.

In each of the massive turrets the gun crews anxiously stood by their 14-inch rifles, already loaded, primed, and aimed at their targets on the distant shore. The dark night sky slowly became lighter, and at H-Hour minus 40 minutes, or 5:50 A.M., just as the dawn was breaking, Captain Baker turned to Buglemaster 2nd Class Will John

Eddleman and gave him the order, "Sound Commence Firing." The young petty officer moistened his lips, pushed the transmit button on the 1MC, or ship's intercom system, and played the bugle call to commence firing.[14]

Commander Richard B. Derickson, the gunnery officer on the old dreadnought, was at his station in the armored conning tower. As the bugle sounded, he gave the order "Commence firing," and the ten 14-inch guns of the *Texas* roared, signaling the commencement of the invasion of Omaha Beach. It was the most memorable moment of Commander Derickson's life. The liberation of Nazi-occupied Europe had begun.[15]

The primary mission of the *Texas* was to neutralize and destroy a battery of German guns reported to be emplaced on the top of Pointe du Hoc, a prominent cliff with a commanding view of both Omaha and Utah beaches. Beginning at 5:50 A.M., the *Texas* rained death and destruction in the form of 14-inch shells on Pointe du Hoc until 6:30, when the ground troops were scheduled to hit the beach. Captain Baker ordered "Cease Fire" at that time, then moved the *Texas* in closer to the beach, dropping the anchor 10,000 yards from shore, where he awaited call for fire missions from the Shore Fire Control Party, due to land at 7:27 A.M. Between 5:50 and 6:24, the *Texas* fired 255 14-inch shells at the casemates and gun positions on Pointe du Hoc.[16]

The firing of the *Texas* did not go unnoticed by the troops going ashore. Sgt. John Slaughter, a mortar section leader in D Company, 116th Infantry Regiment, 29th Infantry Division, recalled, "It was a terrible ride into the beach. Over to our right, the battleship *Texas* was firing into the cliffs, and every time that big 14-inch gun went off, a tremendous tsunami swamped our boat, and the water would come over the side and just soak us and make our seasickness worse."[17]

The German artillery battery reported to be on top of Pointe du Hoc was a group of powerful 6-inch guns, capable of throwing their destructive shells ten miles or more. They could fire on both the American landing beaches, Utah and Omaha, and the guns were powerful enough to sink the Navy transport ships full of

Army soldiers. Because of its potential to disrupt or halt the Allied landing, the Army invasion planners designated Pointe du Hoc as Army Target 1.[18]

To absolutely ensure the destruction of the 6-inch guns on top of Pointe du Hoc, a group of U.S. Army Rangers had a special, almost suicidal, mission in their assault on Omaha Beach. Specially trained American commandos of Companies D, E, and F of the 2nd Ranger Battalion had the incredibly daunting task of climbing Pointe du Hoc, a sheer cliff 110 feet high, and making sure the German artillery at the top of the cliff was destroyed.

The Rangers, under the command of Lt. Col. James Earl Rudder from Eden, Texas, landed at the base of Pointe du Hoc and fired rockets attached to grappling hooks over the top of the cliff. Ropes trailed from the grappling hooks, and once the hooks and ropes went over the tops of the cliffs, the Rangers began climbing. Of course the Germans at the top of the cliff did not stand idly by. In the words of a Marine observer on the *Texas*, Lt. Weldon James, "the Rangers caught hell. Six of their landing craft were swamped or sunk by mortar barrage, and, when they finally reached the beach, they were met with a devastating crossfire. The first grappling ropes, that the Rangers fired over the bluffs, were cut by the Germans sending the climbing men tumbling down the sheer rocky cliffs. The Rangers, exposed on the beach, were showered with hand grenades from above."[19]

Sailors aboard the *Texas* could clearly see the soldiers climbing up the ropes. Some of them were single ropes, while others were rope ladders, swaying back and forth, swinging underneath the cliff face, and back out into the open. The sailors could also see the Germans at the top of the cliff shooting down at the American soldiers. Occasionally they would see one of the rope ladders fall, as if someone had cut the ropes at the top of the cliff. But despite their heavy losses, eventually, with gunfire support from the *Texas* and other ships, the Rangers succeeded in climbing the brutal cliffs of Pointe du Hoc, where they killed or captured the German defenders.[20]

After Captain Baker ordered a cease fire on Pointe du Hoc, the *Texas* fired at numerous targets of opportunity. The targets were located by the Spitfire spotter aircraft flying out of England and relayed to the *Texas*. During the morning of June 6, the *Texas* fired on pillboxes, machinegun nests, and mobile field artillery batteries at the direction of the airborne spotters. Enemy vehicles, troops, and ammunition dumps fell victim to the powerful and accurate 14-inch guns. The secondary battery of 5-inch guns was also active, taking out enemy troop concentrations, machineguns, snipers, and tanks that ventured too near the hotly-contested Omaha Beach. During the course of the day, the 14-inch guns fired some 441 high-capacity and armor piercing shells, while the secondary battery of 5-inch guns added 253 shells to the one-day total.[21]

During the morning of June 6, there was so much dust and smoke from the naval bombardment that the men on the *Texas* could not see the Army troops actually go ashore. The heavily laden landing craft seemed simply to disappear into the "fog of war," as they chugged toward Omaha Beach. Occasionally the sailors could see the flash from an explosion, but there was little else to indicate what was going on ashore, or who was winning the battle.

As the landing craft shuttled back and forth between the beach and the transport ships containing more Army troops, Allied aircraft filled the skies overhead. By 11:00 A.M. the smoke and dust enveloping the beach had cleared sufficiently to allow the men on the deck of the *Texas* to observe the beach-head battleground. The sailors could clearly see soldiers moving about on the shore, as well as the landing craft unloading at the edge of the beach, as more soldiers joined the battle.[22]

Omaha Beach was about 7,500 yards wide and about 100 to 150 yards deep. Behind the beach was a steep cliff. To move inland from Omaha Beach, the Army troops had to go through one of two beach exits, each of which consisted of a gulley or ravine, through which ran a small road or trail. The gulley at the left end of the beach led to the town of Colleville-sur-mer, while the gulley at the right end led to Vierville-sur-mer. German snipers and machinegunners hid in the houses lying alongside the gullies and fired on the American troops

Wounded U.S. Army Rangers alongside the Texas.

Wounded Rangers being cared for on the Texas.

attempting to exit the beach, especially at the Vierville exit. After being informed of the situation by the Spitfire spotter aircraft shortly after noon, Captain Baker moved the *Texas* to within 3,000 yards of the shore and at this point-blank range flattened every house along the Vierville road (known as Exit D-1) with devastating 14-inch gunfire. Several destroyers joined with the *Texas* in clearing out the area. As soon as the *Texas* and other ships ceased firing, Army engineers using bulldozers quickly built up a ramp where the road had been, and American troops began moving rapidly from the beach-head inland into the surrounding countryside.

During the afternoon, the spotters in the foretop of the *Texas* continued to find targets for the 5-inch broadside guns. Using the exceptionally accurate 5-inch guns as large, long-range sniper rifles, the spotters fired on pillboxes, tanks, machineguns, and enemy snipers.[23]

As daylight faded on this most momentous of days, the *Texas* darkened ship and prepared for an eventful night. During the night Captain Baker received an alert of an enemy air raid, and at about midnight the crew began to see anti-aircraft fire in all directions. Captain Baker ordered his men not to fire at any enemy aircraft unless it came within one thousand yards of the ship. The captain reasoned that firing at airplanes would immediately give away the location of the ship, and firing at night without radar guidance is inaccurate in any case. So the *Texas* did not fire during that long night, although the crewmembers on deck did see several planes going down in flames in the skies nearby. Several times during this and subsequent nights, the *Texas* was the unintended recipient of friendly anti-aircraft fire. What goes up must come down, and whenever other ships fired at enemy planes, their shells sometimes struck the *Texas*.[24]

The crew remained at their battle stations all night long, and the radio counter-measure team detected several German radio-guided missiles. With their special radio transmitters, the counter-measure team jammed the radio receivers of the German missiles, and the lookouts reported seeing two of the radio-guided missiles splashing into the sea several hundred yards from the *Texas*. Another of the

German missiles smashed into the destroyer U.S.S. *Meridith*, causing the ship to sink the following day.[25]

On June 7, the second day of the invasion, the destroyer U.S.S. *Harding* notified the *Texas* that the Ranger force at Pointe du Hoc was in dire straits and was in immediate need of replacement weapons, ammunition, and food. Additionally, a number of wounded soldiers needing immediate medical attention had gathered at the foot of the cliff. Captain Baker obtained two Landing Craft, Vehicle and Personnel (LCVPs) and brought them alongside the *Texas*, where he instructed his sailors to place on the craft 30-caliber ammunition, food, and water. He then sent the LCVPs to the beach at Pointe du Hoc. After delivering their badly needed cargo, the coxswains of the landing craft returned to the *Texas* bearing forty-one wounded Rangers, one dead Coast Guardsman, and twenty-seven prisoners of war. Of the last, twenty were Germans, including one officer, four were Italians, and three were French.[26]

Every *Texas* sailor who was not otherwise occupied came out on the deck to see and honor the wounded Rangers, and the Marine Detachment turned out in force to guard the prisoners. As the wounded came aboard, one of the ship's doctors was on the main deck, and he determined who needed treatment immediately, and who could wait. The most seriously wounded went to the operating room where the senior surgeon administered to their injuries. One of the junior surgeons set up a secondary operating room on the third deck directly below sick bay. The ship's crew willingly gave up their bunks for the recuperation of the wounded. Of the forty-one wounded soldiers brought aboard, only one died of his injuries, suffering from severe abdominal wounds.[27] The remaining Rangers stoically suffered their wounds in silence, and the crew of the *Texas* would have agreed with Gen. Omar Bradley when he said, "Every man who set foot on Omaha Beach that day was a hero."[28]

One of the wounded soldiers was PFC Clarence Bachman, of Company E, 2nd Ranger Battalion. He had been shot by a concealed sniper on June 6, the bullet entering his back near the spine, while he was on top of the cliff. After initial treatment by an Army medic ashore, Bachman was placed on the LCVP and sent to the *Texas*. He came aboard the old battlewagon in a Stokes basket, and the ship's doctor performed surgery on him in the ship's operating room on the second deck.

After being treated, the wounded Rangers spent the night on the *Texas*, then the following day they went aboard a British ship for movement to England. Once in the British Isles, the soldiers went to various hospitals for recovery, but they always retained a warm place in their hearts for the U.S.S. *Texas*, their place of refuge and care.[29]

As their duties permitted during the days following June 6, many of the ship's officers and sailors came up to the main deck to have a look around at what for the majority of the men was the most significant day of their lives. Among those who came out on the deck was Doctor Hanlon, the senior medical officer on the ship. Looking out at the scenes of combat and destruction, he became angry at the sight of so many American bodies floating in the water. He assigned Pharmacist's Mate James Naismith and another sailor to pull as many bodies as possible out of the water, so they could be treated with respect and prevented from simply washing out to sea. Naismith saw one body floating by with its face down, only a helmet, shoulders, and hands showing. Something was gripped in the hands. Naismith and another sailor seized the body with a boathook and drug it up onto the flat surface of the anti-torpedo blister where they were standing. They found that the dead man had the steering wheel of an LCM clutched tightly in his hands. His whole face was blown away. His dog tags were still attached, and the two sailors tried to get his hands off of the LCM wheel. When they pried his hands loose from the wheel, they found a crucifix, the chain of which was wrapped around the fingers of one hand. Naismith took the crucifix from his hand and placed it around the dead man's neck, along with his dog tags. He hoped that the crucifix would be included with the personal effects of the dead man when they were shipped back to his family.[30]

On June 7 and 8 the *Texas* continued to support the Army troops ashore by firing at enemy positions, and at night the American ships off the shore of Normandy came under increasingly heavy air attack.

At 6:30 in the morning of June 9, Captain Baker received orders to leave the assault area and proceed to Plymouth, England, to replenish the ship's exhausted supply of fuel and ammunition. The old dreadnought moored in Plymouth Harbor just after 10:00 p.m. and spent the remainder of the 9th and all of the 10th of June taking on fuel and ammunition, and also repairing the minor damage caused by the ship's own gunfire. After returning to the invasion beach on June 11, the *Texas* stood by, ready to provide gunfire support as needed.[31]

The final fire mission of the *Texas* at Omaha beach occurred on the morning of June 15. Elements of the First U.S. Army had located a large concentration of German troops assembling between Isigny and Carentan, and requested 14-inch fire from the *Texas*. The range to the target was in excess of 20,000 yards, beyond the normal range for old dreadnought. To overcome the distance barrier, Captain Baker ordered the flooding of the starboard blisters, in order to induce a two-degree starboard list to the ship. This action allowed the 14-inch guns to elevate to seventeen degrees, giving her the additional range to reach the German troops. Employing air spotters, the *Texas* began lobbing her 14-inch high-capacity projectiles at 6:30 A.M., killing many of the German soldiers and scattering the survivors. After this last fire mission, the American troops had advanced inland beyond the range of the *Texas*, and the services of the battlewagon were no longer needed.[32]

The outcome of the Allied invasion of German-occupied France was by no means a sure thing. The stubborn defense by the Germans held up the American infantry on the beaches for a considerable time, and the courageous American troops suffered many casualties. Without their own artillery and with very few tanks ashore, the Army soldiers depended on the Navy for gunfire support. The big guns of the *Texas* and other ships helped to save the day for the American troops ashore. In his autobiography Gen. Omar Bradley wrote: "Here I must give unstinting praise to the U.S. Navy. As on Sicily, the Navy saved our hides." He explained, "the main batteries of these gallant ships became our sole artillery." Bradley also remembered that when Maj. Gen. Leonard T. Gerow arrived ashore on the evening of D-Day to establish his V-Corps command posts, his first emotional message back to the command ship was "Thank God for the U.S. Navy!"[33]

CHAPTER EIGHT

Cherbourg and Southern France

On June 18 the *Texas* once again departed the invasion coast along with fellow dreadnoughts *Arkansas* and *Nevada* and sailed for Plymouth, England, mooring in the Plymouth Harbor that night. During the next few days the old battlewagon replenished her supply of fuel and ammunition, and then sailed to Portland on the 21st, to stand ready to assist the Army in its attack on the French port city of Cherbourg. Over the next few days, many of the crew enjoyed liberty ashore, and on Saturday, June 24, all the divisions of the ship had their photographs taken on the forecastle.[1]

After the initial invasion of France at Normandy, getting military supplies ashore to the troops who needed them was an arduous process. Supply ships anchored some distance away from the beach at Normandy, and then sailors on board the ships had to transfer the supplies to landing craft. The landing craft then chugged in to the beach, where soldiers and sailors unloaded the vessels and placed the needed material in supply dumps until it could be removed by trucks. This was a time-consuming, physically demanding ordeal, and not enough supplies were getting ashore quickly enough for the use of the Army troops fighting the Germans.

To alleviate the supply situation, Allied forces needed to capture a port, and the best candidate was at Cherbourg. Capturing the port at Cherbourg was essential to keeping up the supply of men and material needed to continue the offensive begun at Normandy and to push the German Army out of France. But the German Army occupied the city of Cherbourg, and part of the defenses included several batteries of large artillery emplaced in heavily fortified concrete installations. The U.S. Army VII Corps requested naval bombardment of the German artillery.

At 3:40 in the morning of Sunday, June 25, the *Texas* got underway from Portland Harbor and sailed toward Cherbourg to bombard the shore installations there and to furnish gunfire support while the U.S. 4th Infantry Division attacked the town. Sailing with the *Texas* was the *Arkansas*, as well as the destroyers *Barton*, *O'Brien*, and *Laffey*, and several minesweepers. This group of ships comprised Task Group 129.2, under the command of Rear Admiral Carleton F. Bryant on the *Texas*.[2]

The Germans had heavily mined the waters approaching Cherbourg Harbor, so the tiny minesweepers led the American armada into the area. At 9:15 A.M. Captain Baker sounded General Quarters, and all hands moved quickly to their battle stations. The Army had requested that the bombardment group open fire at 10:30, but because the exact location of friendly lines ashore was uncertain, Admiral Bryant decided to change the bombardment plan. He ordered the ships to only fire at the request of Army Shore Fire Control Parties, or to return the fire of coastal batteries when fired upon. Meanwhile, spotter planes flying over the German artillery emplacements reported that there was no enemy activity near the guns and that one of the targets was surrounded by dead Germans.[3] The dead Germans apparently came to life, for at 12:29 the minesweepers and their escorting destroyers came under heavy-caliber fire from the German batteries. One salvo straddled the *Barton*, while the splash from another salvo completely enveloped one of the minesweepers. The third salvo was a straddle across the bow of the *Texas*. The distance to the shore at this time was 8,000 to 10,000

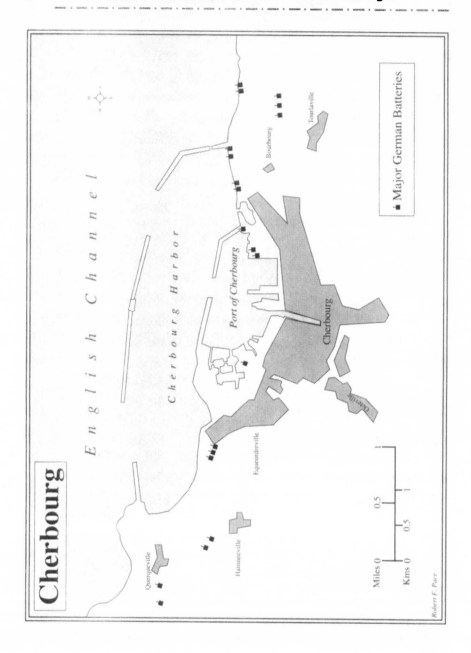

yards, and haze and smoke made it difficult to see the shore. For several minutes Captain Baker could not be sure where the enemy fire originated, and the spotter planes had difficulty locating the German guns that were firing. Captain Baker commenced maneuvering to open the range and avoid the German shells, while the spotter plane tried to find the offending guns. At 12:39 the *Texas* opened fire using target coordinates given by the spotter plane. Finally sailors in the foretop observed the gun flashes, and Captain Baker shifted fire to the visible target.[4]

Enemy shells continued to straddle the *Texas*, landing with alarming frequency and proximity. Several shell splashes sent geysers of water up to the level of the admiral's bridge, some eighty feet above the water line. The deck of the battleship was drenched from the splashes of the near-misses. To offer some protection for the *Texas*, Admiral Bryant ordered the destroyers to lay smoke between the battleship and the shore. This action reduced the fire of the German batteries, but a continuous eight knot wind quickly blew the smoke away.[5]

At 1:00 P.M. the *Texas* turned once again toward the shore to close the distance between the battleship and the minesweepers, which were being fired upon by the German shore batteries. Continuously firing the ship's 14-inch guns, the *Texas* came under increasingly heavy fire as she came closer to the coast. Chaplain Moody, on the bridge telling the crew about the events over the ship's intercom system, had the feeling that the ship would be hit and that his time had come.[6]

Captain Baker was a very busy man, running out onto the wings of the bridge to see where the German shells were landing, then coming back into the bridge to give orders to the helmsman. The destroyers were laying smoke in an effort to hide the ships from the shore batteries, and the *Texas* and *Arkansas* were both twisting and turning, trying to stay cloaked within the protective smoke screen, while also trying not to collide with each other or one of the smaller ships. As one of the destroyers raced by, it flashed a message with its signal lamp: "Come on, *Texas*," the old battle cry of the aging dreadnought.

German shells narrowly miss the Texas.

The Texas *fires at German shore batteries.*

The air spotter had the German guns definitely located and called in corrections in an attempt to put the 14-inch shells of the *Texas* on top of the enemy artillery.[7]

There was a big splash and explosion just off the starboard bow as one of the German shells narrowly missed the *Texas*. Chaplain Moody put his microphone down on the chart table in the navigation bridge and stepped forward so he was beside the helmsman, Quartermaster 3rd Class Christen Christiansen. "That's a close one, wasn't it, Chris?" The helmsman replied, "Sure was, Chaplain." Then Chaplain Moody walked back to the chart table and picked up his microphone in his hand.[8]

Buglemaster 2nd Class Will John Eddleman was watching the radar scope on the bridge, because the smokescreen made it impossible to see the nearby ships. The captain had just stepped back into the bridge from the starboard wing when Eddleman said, "Captain, there's a large blip on the PPI, I believe it to be the *Arkansas*, about two points off our starboard bow." He had to yell to make himself heard above the din of the shells bursting nearby, and the guns of the *Texas* firing in reply. Captain Baker gave the order to the helmsman to steer hard right and get out of harm's way. Christiansen answered up, "Helm hard right, sir."[9]

At 1:16 P.M. a deafening roar enveloped the bridge and filled the space with a thick, choking, brown smoke. A 240-millimeter German shell had landed on top of the armored conning tower, eight feet below the navigation bridge. The shell skidded along the top of the conning tower, shearing off the gun director periscope in the conning tower, then striking the supporting column of the navigation bridge and detonating there. The blast completely destroyed the forward part of the bridge, peeling back the steel deck plates and causing the sheared-off rivets to fly about inside the bridge like machinegun bullets.

The explosion blew Chaplain Moody up on top of the chart table, tangling him in wiring while flying shrapnel dented his helmet. Eddleman, temporarily knocked unconscious, came to lying on the deck, his face burning from contact with the deck plates heated by the explosion. Several other men who were inside the crowded bridge were knocked down or momentarily stunned by the explosion. Captain Baker, who had been just outside the starboard bridge door out on the starboard wing, stuck his head back inside the bridge and called out, "All hands below." Most of the able-bodied then fled the bridge, leaving the mayhem and destruction behind them.[10]

Chaplain Moody, Buglemaster Eddleman, Captain Baker's Marine orderly Private Buckout, and Lieutenant Commander Spear, the navigator, all remained behind to aid the wounded. The helmsman, Quartermaster 3rd Class Christiansen, was the most severely wounded as he had been standing right above the spot where the German shell exploded. One of his legs had been traumatically amputated, the other had a compound fracture, and he had other severe injuries. Christiansen quickly lapsed into unconsciousness and died shortly after the explosion. Five other men in the bridge were badly injured, wounded by the deck plates of the bridge as they peeled back, or by the flying rivets.[11]

Hospital corpsmen and stretcher bearers hurried to the bridge and removed the dying and wounded, as Captain Baker carried on the fight from his new post inside the armored conning tower. German shells continued to explode alongside the *Texas*, and geysers of water rained down upon the decks as the rescue party took the injured sailors below to sickbay. After being hit, the *Texas* kept up its fire on the German coastal batteries with no interruption from 1:16 P.M. until ordered to retire by Admiral Bryant at 3:00 P.M. During that time, the dreadnought fired 206 rounds of 14-inch ammunition at the enemy.[12] In reply, the German guns fired approximately sixty-five shells that either straddled or narrowly missed the *Texas*.

At one point during the exchange of gunfire between the battleship and the German shore batteries, the *Texas* turned so that her stern was pointed toward the German guns. Turret five fired directly astern, an unusual act, as ships almost always fired with the guns trained out to the side, rather than pointed directly ahead or aft. Friendly air cover had been provided by planes flying from England and no enemy aircraft were expected, so canvas covers protected the 40-millimeter ready ammunition stored in brackets on the inside of the quad-40 gun tubs. When the 14-inch guns of turret five fired, the ball of flame emitted from the huge muzzles ignited the canvas ammunition covers.

Men from the Marine detachment of the *Texas* manned the two quad-40 anti-aircraft guns at the stern of the ship. Sergeant Major

Liila was the battery officer for the aft quad-40 on the port side. When the German shells began exploding near the *Texas*, the sergeant major ordered his men to seek protection between turrets four and five. When the canvas covers over the 40-millimeter ammunition caught fire, he was concerned that the ammunition might explode, so he ordered his Marines to throw the ammunition over the side of the ship. The Marines rushed forward to dispose of the ammunition, as Sergeant Major Liila kept track of the time between the 14-inch salvos. When it was time for the *Texas* to fire, he called the Marines back to safety so they would not be injured by the concussion of the blast of the big guns. Between shots, the Marines threw the hot 40-millimeter shells over the side, while sailors extinguished the burning canvas covers.[13] Two of the sailors fighting the fire were caught out on the deck during one of the salvos and suffered from concussions as a result of the blast.

While the battle raged between the *Texas* and the German coastal artillery, a second shell struck the *Texas* but did not explode. This shell, discovered by a damage control party at 2:47 P.M., struck the port side of the ship at frame 19, about twelve feet down from the main deck. The projectile, a 240-millimeter high-capacity shell with a base fuse, entered the ship in a nose down attitude, apparently flying sideways, rather than with the point forward. The shell came to rest in the state-room of Warrant Officer M.A. Clark. When the damage control party discovered the unexploded ordnance, they stuffed mattresses around it to keep it from rolling about and then vacated the area.

The gunfire exchange continued, but eventually the German installations were distroyed. After the duel with the German shore batteries at Cherbourg the *Texas* returned to England, and went to the U.S. Naval Advanced Amphibious Base at Portland, arriving there in the early morning hours of June 26. During the trip, Captain Baker summoned the ship's bomb disposal officer, Lieutenant Ford, and instructed him to take a look at the shell in order to disarm it. Lieutenant Ford examined the shell, then told Captain Baker that he was not familiar with the fuse and had no information on it. Captain Baker instructed Ford not to attempt to disarm the fuse, but to await help from the experts at Portland. When the ship anchored in Portland, Captain Baker alerted the harbormaster that he needed a bomb disposal officer.

Lt. Stephen A. Sturdevant was asleep in his quarters when a messenger awakened him and told him that he was needed aboard the *Texas*. Lieutenant Sturdevant went to the dock where he was told there was an unexploded shell aboard the ship. Sturdevant then went out to the anchorage of the *Texas* and was met on board by Lieutenant Ford, the ship's bomb disposal officer, and Commander Cabanillas, the executive officer. Many members of the crew were sleeping on the main deck when the bomb disposal officer went aboard because the area adjacent to the unexploded shell had been evacuated. Lieutenant Ford and Commander Cabanillas took Lieutenant Sturdevant below to the cabin of Warrant Officer Clark. The German shell was resting on the deck at frame 19 near where it entered the ship. Commander Cabanillas then went about his duties and left the two lieutenants to deal with the shell.

Lieutenants Sturdevant and Ford wedged the shell, a 240-millimeter armor-piercing projectile, so that it could not roll and closely examined it, especially the fuse in the base of the shell. Sturdevant had never seen a fuse of that type, but he was the resident expert, so he had to deal with the unfamiliar bomb. From examining the shell and the area where it entered the ship, Sturdevant concluded that the shell had struck the water then ricocheted and tumbled into the ship vertically rather than point first. Sturdevant believed that the ricocheting motion had distorted the action in the fuse and caused it to malfunction. Attempting to remove the fuse in place might have caused it to explode, so the two officers rigged a sling around the shell and with a working party muscled it into a passageway, then along the passageway and got it under a hatch. The men then hoisted the shell up to the main deck and over the side into a LCVP, all the while keeping the shell horizontal so as not to disturb the fuse. Lieutenant Sturdevant planned to take the shell out through the breakwater of the harbor and to drop it over the side into deep water.

While slowly motoring out to the breakwater, Sturdevant discovered that the fuse was loose in the fuse pocket, so he carefully removed the fuse. This action made the shell much more stable and less dangerous, so the party returned to the *Texas* and put the shell back aboard. Sturdevant then made an impression of the base plug and had a machinist make a spanner wrench to match the impression. With the newly-made wrench, Lieutenant Sturdevant removed the base plug, exposing the cast explosive charge inside. Then he took the shell ashore and cautiously steamed the explosive out of the shell. He also disassembled the fuse and found that the striker had impinged the primer, but the primer did not explode.

After Lieutenant Sturdevant took the shell ashore, the *Texas* sailed to Plymouth for repairs, but after a few days Lieutenant Ford came back to Portland and reclaimed the shell as a trophy for the *Texas*.

For his actions in not only removing the shell, but also removing the fuse, detonator, and explosive from the shell in order to obtain intelligence about the German weapon, Lt. Stephen Allen Sturdevant received the Bronze Star Medal with Combat "V".[13] Lieutenant Sturdevant earned a medal, and the *Texas* gained a souvenir.

After the action at Cherbourg, the crew took up a collection and purchased a one thousand dollar war bond for the widow of the helmsman Chris Christiansen. The crew also gave bonds to the other more seriously wounded men, some of whom would never fully recover from their injuries.[15]

After spending only a few hours in Portland, the *Texas* sailed to the Devonport Dockyard at Plymouth, England, to repair the damage sustained at Cherbourg. Yard workers completed the ship's repairs on July 3, and Captain Baker determined that the vessel was ready for sea. The following day, the Fourth of July, the *Texas* got underway for Belfast Lough, Northern Ireland, where it anchored on July 5. She stayed at Belfast for the next ten days, taking on stores and fuel, and reinstalling the ship's catapult that had been removed prior to the invasion of France.

On the night of July 15, shortly before midnight, the dreadnought got underway for Taranto, Italy, as the guide of Task Group 120.8.

The floor of the navigation bridge after the explosion.

Where the helmsman was standing.

Where the dud entered the ship.

*Admiral Bryant and Captain Baker with the
German shell that did not explode.*

Other ships in the task group included the British carriers H.M.S. *Emperor*, *Khedive*, *Searcher*, and *Pursuer*, and the anti-aircraft cruiser H.M.S. *Ulster Queen*. During the next few days as the task group steamed south, the carriers regularly exercised their aircraft, while the escorting destroyers searched the depths for submarines. The task group entered the Straits of Gibraltar during the night of July 21, shortly before midnight, and steamed into the Mediterranean Sea.

The first leg of the dreadnought's journey ended as the ship moored in the Mers El Keber harbor at Oran in French North Africa on July 23. On the 27th the ship was underway again, and on July 30 she arrived at the harbor of Taranto, Italy.[16] During the first several days of August, the *Texas* remained berthed in Taranto Harbor, while the officers briefed the crew about their duties in the upcoming Operation Anvil, the invasion of Southern France.

Their short stay in Italy was not entirely enjoyable for the crew. The officers warned the *Texas* sailors not to drink the local water, eat any of the local food, or visit any of the local barbershops. The one bright spot during their time in Taranto was a United Services Organization, or USO, show enjoyed by the crew. Entertainers Jack Healy, Mary Brien, and several other young ladies sang for the crew on a stage improvised on the forecastle. These were the first American civilians, and more importantly, American girls, that the crew had seen for several months.[17]

Allied military planners had long debated the merits of opening a second front in France, on the Mediterranean coast of the country. Some of the planners, especially the Americans, believed that such an effort would have the following results: it would weaken the German defense of Northern France; it would allow the Allies to use Marseilles, the largest port in France; and it would permit the Allies to use the Rhone Valley rail and road network, enabling the rapid transport of troops and supplies. Opponents of the plan, including British Prime Minister Winston Churchill, argued that such an invasion would weaken the Allied effort in Italy, which by the summer of 1944 had deteriorated into a slow, grinding, war of attrition heavily favoring the German defenders in the Italian mountains.

Lacking a clear consensus, the Combined Chiefs of Staff cancelled the invasion of the French Mediterranean coast, code-named Operation Anvil, and focused their efforts on the invasion of Normandy. After the successful invasion of northern France in Operation Overlord, the initial rapid movement of the Allied armies soon slowed to a crawl as U.S. and British forces slogged through the tough and heavily-defended hedgerow country of France. The need to resurrect Operation Anvil became evident, and the Allied command approved the assault, to be carried out by the U.S. Seventh Army. The name of the operation was changed from Anvil to Dragoon, supposedly because Prime Minister Churchill complained of being "dragooned" or coerced into approving the plan.[18]

The initial invasion force consisted of the U.S. 3rd, 36th, and 45th Infantry Divisions under the overall command of VI Corps commander Maj. Gen. Lucian Truscott. Allied planners decided to center the assault on the area around St. Tropez, some thirty miles east of Toulon. The beachhead was fairly extensive, consisting of about fifty miles of shoreline. The immediate objective for the Army infantry was the capture of the ports at Toulon and Marseilles.[19]

In accordance with the invasion plan, the *Texas* departed Taranto Harbor at 3:00 P.M. on August 11 and began steaming for the invasion beaches on the southern coast of France. Sailing with the *Texas* was the battleship *Nevada*, the cruiser *Philadelphia*, and the French cruisers *Montcalm* and *George Leygues*, and a squadron of American destroyers. During the evening of August 14, the *Texas* completed a rendezvous with other Allied ships of the invasion force, then continued on its way to the ship's fire support station, just off the invasion beaches. At dusk the crew went to their air defense stations and at dawn went to general quarters.

The primary target for the *Texas*, designated Target P-39, was a five-gun battery of German 220-millimeter guns emplaced in rock casemates. At about 4:40 A.M. the crew could hear the sounds of heavy explosions in the invasion area as bombers of the Army Air Forces dropped their deadly loads on and behind the beaches. By 5:00 A.M., the *Texas* was in its assigned position, waiting for enough

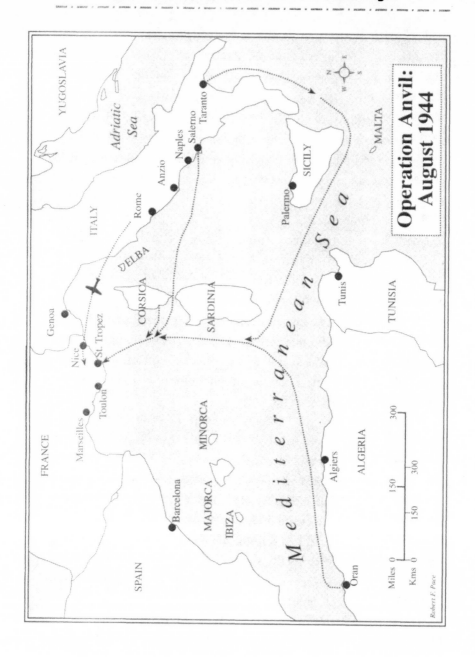

Operation Anvil: August 1944

daylight to see the targets, to begin the bombardment. As dawn broke over the target area, the spotters in the foremast noticed that the coast was obscured by low-lying clouds, haze, and smoke from the heavy bombing. When the spotter aircraft from the *Texas* flew over the target areas, they could not see their targets because of the clouds, dust and smoke.[20]

At 6:32 A.M. the lookouts observed gunfire splashes in the water about one thousand yards ahead of the *Texas*, and a few minutes later Captain Baker received word that Target P-39 was firing. The airplane spotter could not see the enemy guns because of the low-lying clouds, and the spotters on the ship could not see the land at all. At 6:51 the *Texas* opened fire using radar to locate the German battery, but the pilot in the circling Kingfisher could not see where the 14-inch shells landed. The ship then fired a salvo of two shots each from turrets one, three, and five, which rocked the ship, but the pilot still could not see where the shots landed. Admiral Bryant then ordered the destroyer *Fitch* to move in as close as possible to the shore, in an attempt to spot the fall of the shot from the *Texas*. This action was successful, and the *Fitch* reported that the gunfire from the *Texas* was right on target. With the knowledge that the shells were landing in the right area, the *Texas* fired a salvo from all ten 14-inch guns, causing dust and paint chips to fly in many of the compartments below deck.[21]

The troops landed on time at 8:00 A.M., but as the *Texas'* primary target was several miles away from the initial landing site, the battleship continued to fire on the German guns, raining down death and destruction with 14-inch projectiles. Shortly after the U.S. soldiers began storming the beach, a second destroyer, the *Emmons*, advised the *Texas* that the gunfire was "most effectively" covering the target. At 8:15 the *Texas* ceased fire in accordance with the bombardment plan, having fired 172 rounds of 14-inch ammunition in one hour and twenty-four minutes.[22] During the rest of the day the dreadnought remained in gunfire support position, awaiting a call for fire missions from shore fire control parties. As the battle ashore progressed, the U.S. Army forces quickly overran the German positions and did not require gunfire support from the *Texas* for the rest of the day.

Late that evening, at about 8:55 P.M., a flight of four German Heinkel-111 bombers flew out over the invasion fleet and one of them approached the *Texas*. When the plane flew within approximately 6,500 yards, anti-aircraft gunners on the battleship opened fire. Sailors manning five of the 3-inch guns and five of the 40-millimeter mounts delivered a withering fire, causing the German plane to take evasive action and turn away, after which it disappeared from sight. At ten that night the crew stood down from general quarters, by which time there were a great number of tired, hungry, hot, and dirty sailors, suffering in the sweltering Mediterranean summer heat. During the night the *Texas* steamed at sea, returning to the fire support area before daylight.[23]

During the day of August 16, the *Texas* stood by ready to provide gunfire support to the Army, but the lack of serious German opposition prevented any targets being assigned to the old dreadnought. By 7:00 P.M. it was apparent that the Army would not need assistance from the 14-inch guns of the battlewagon, and the *Texas* retired to the night assembly area. During the night, at 3:30 in the morning of August 17, Admiral Carleton Bryant, Commander Task Group 85.12, ordered the battleship to depart the area and proceed to Palermo, Sicily.

The role of the *Texas* in the invasion of Southern France had ended. The success of the battleship's efforts is evidenced by the fact that the German artillery did not fire between the time of the *Texas'* first salvo and the capture of the German guns by elements of the U.S. 3rd Infantry Division. The aging dreadnought once again proved its value and contributed to the success of American troops ashore.

After a brief stop in Palermo, the *Texas*, along with the *Arkansas*, steamed to Algiers, the capital city of Algeria, where the two old dreadnoughts were joined by a third, the *Nevada*. After spending several days at Algiers, the *Texas* and *Nevada* sailed on to Oran, Algeria. On September 4 the three battleships, comprising Battleship Division

Five, received the welcome orders from Commander Eighth Fleet to sail to the U.S. The ships got underway just after nine in the morning, to the great relief and joy of the crew.[24] Admiral Bryant, Commander Battleship Division Five, sent the following message to the men of the *Texas*:

> We are on our way home after a job well done. When you go on your well earned leave relax and enjoy yourselves to the utmost but don't boast and don't broadcast any information of a technical nature. While these invasions have given us plenty of action let no one belittle the escorting of troop convoys by ships of BatDiv 5. The battle of the Atlantic has really been a battle. You not only saw to it that the troops got safely across the Atlantic but you saw to it that they were landed safely in enemy held territory. That is a record of which we all can be justly proud. After our overhaul there will be more for us to do. The Germans are nearly out of the picture. With the help of BatDiv 5 the Japs will be eliminated.[25]

The battle-tested sailors of the *Texas* were headed home again, after three major battles and sustaining their first combat casualties. The boys who had left home several months before were now men and combat veterans. They would never be the same.

CHAPTER NINE

Lone Star of Suribachi— The U.S.S. *Texas* at Iwo Jima

The *Texas* arrived at the New York Navy Yard on the morning of September 14 and spent the next several weeks undergoing repairs and a general overhaul, which included two weeks in dry dock.[1] Improvements to the ship included replacing the barrels on the 14-inch rifles, which had far exceeded their service lives of 200 to 250 rounds per barrel. The Navy placed one of the gun barrels on a trailer and put it on display in New York City as the centerpiece of a War Bond drive.

After the completion of repairs, Captain Baker once again took his ship to sea, and the *Texas* experienced the routine post-dry dock trials and speed tests. While in New York the battleship received many new sailors, and these men as well as the ship herself were put through their paces during the next several days. The crew practiced launching and recovering aircraft, as well as firing all the various guns on board. Drills practiced by the crew included collision, fire, damage control, abandon ship, and general quarters. In early November the *Texas* passed her annual military inspection, conducted by the new

One of the 14-inch gun barrels from the Texas.

commander of Battleship Division Five, Rear Admiral I.C. Sowell, while berthed at Casco Bay, Maine.

November 11, 1944, was celebrated as Armistice Day, or the day the First World War ended. On that day the *Texas* got underway in company with the *Arkansas* and two destroyers, forming Task Group 27.7, and sailed for the Panama Canal. On the following day America's newest battleship, the U.S.S. *Missouri*, joined the task group at sea, having just completed her trials, shakedown, and inaugural battle practice. After passing through the multiple locks of the Panama Canal, the *Texas* entered the Pacific Ocean and set sail for Los Angeles Harbor at San Pedro, California, where the ship anchored on November 27.[2]

After conducting various exercises in the area for several days, the *Texas* weighed anchor and got underway on December 3. The destination was Pearl Harbor, Territory of Hawaii. There was no longer any doubt in anyone's mind that the *Texas*, and her crew, would soon be fighting the Japanese.

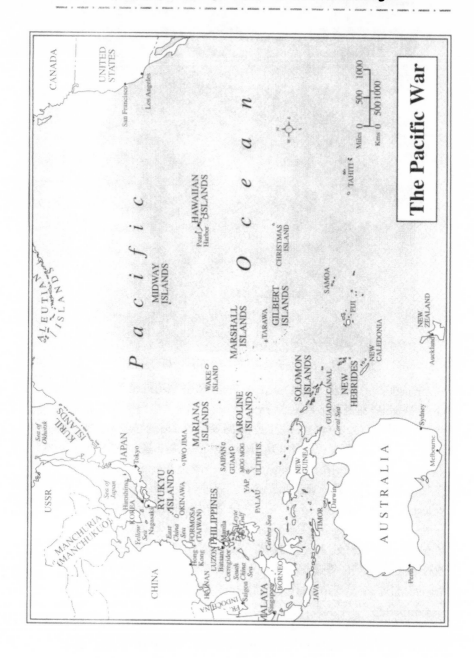

The Pacific War

Once the old dreadnought arrived in Pearl Harbor on December 9, the crew conducted numerous gunnery exercises while the ship received minor repairs. In Pearl Harbor, the crew painted the ship a dark blue, called Measure 21 Camouflage, to make it blend in with the deep blue waters of the Pacific Ocean. The ship and crew celebrated Christmas on Oahu, and many of the men experienced the generous hospitality of the islanders. Marine Ralph Fletcher recalled going to a fancy restaurant in Honolulu on Christmas Eve, where he had a sumptuous and extravagant meal. When the waiter brought the check, the price of the grand dinner was only ten cents. PFC Fletcher told the cashier, "Sir, I believe my check is wrong." The cashier, who was also the manager, looked at the check, then looked up at the Marine and said, "No, it's right. Merry Christmas, Joe." That simple gesture meant a great deal to a young man far from his home and family.[3]

After spending Christmas in Hawaii, the battleship was underway on January 9 and formed up the following day with several other ships of Task Group 52.11, which then sailed to the Ulithi Islands, in the Western Pacific, northwest of New Guinea. Arriving in Ulithi Lagoon on January 23, the crew spent the remainder of January and the first ten days of February taking on stores and supplies, making minor repairs to the ship, and luxuriating in the questionable amenities of Mog Mog Island, in actuality little more than a patch of sand jutting out of the blue Pacific waters, where sailors on liberty could sit on the beach and enjoy two warm beers each day. The seriousness of their situation was brought home to the men when they learned their next assignment was to provide support for Marines assaulting a small volcanic island known as Iwo Jima.

After the catastrophic Japanese attack on American forces at Pearl Harbor on December 7, 1941, the United States was forced to wage a defensive war in the Pacific for many months. American soldiers, sailors, and Marines defended against and slowed the advance of the brutal Japanese in the battles of Wake, Guam, and the Philippines, while gathering strength for the inevitable American counter-offensive. U.S. Naval victories at Coral Sea and Midway led to the first

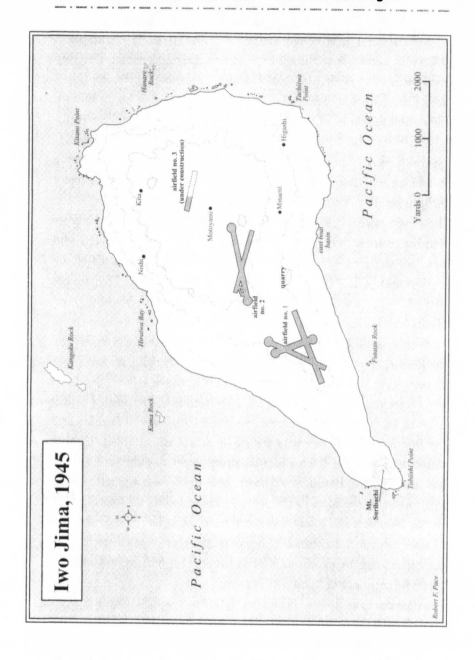

Iwo Jima, 1945

American ground offensive of World War II at Guadalcanal, in the Solomon Islands northeast of Australia. The eventual American success there led to other U.S. offensive operations, and in 1943 and 1944 American forces pushed the Japanese Army and Navy back closer and closer to the Japanese home islands.

The war in the Pacific evolved into a two-pronged thrust, one through the islands of the Central Pacific, with the other moving through the South and Southwest Pacific. Admiral Chester W. Nimitz, Commander in Chief, U.S. Pacific Fleet and Pacific Ocean Areas, commanded U.S. forces in the Central Pacific. Gen. Douglas MacArthur commanded American forces in the South and Southwest Pacific.

By the summer of 1944, Saipan, Tinian, and Guam were in American hands. Massive B-29 Superfortress bombers based on those islands visited death and destruction on Japan in the form of massive air raids. America was closing on Japan, but the ultimate military objective, the forcible invasion of the Japanese home islands, required bases much closer than any islands thus far conquered or liberated. America needed a stepping-stone from which to launch the invasion of Japan itself.

By September 1944, Admiral Nimitz considered the next step in the drive toward Japan and consulted his chief Army and Marine subordinates concerning the matter. These men determined that the most logical and feasible next step in the Pacific war was to seize the island of Iwo Jima and then the much larger island of Okinawa, in the Ryukyu Island chain, south of Japan. The Joint Chiefs of Staff in Washington concurred and issued orders to Admiral Nimitz to seize the islands.[4]

After spending a little more than two weeks at Ulithi Atoll, the *Texas* departed on February 10 and steamed for the island of Tinian, for a rehearsal of Operation Detachment, the amphibious assault of Iwo Jima. After two days of exercises with other ships in the task force, on February 14 the *Texas* began steaming toward the Volcano Islands, the local name for Iwo Jima and its neighbors. Just before midnight on the night of February 15, the radar on the *Texas* picked up Iwo Jima at a distance of sixty-four miles.[5]

A spotter plane from the Texas *with Iwo Jima in the background.*

At 7:00 A.M. on the morning of February 16, spotters in the foremast sighted Mount Suribachi at a range of about twenty thousand yards, or ten nautical miles. Five minutes later Captain Baker ordered the ship's air detachment to begin its spotting mission, and the crew catapulted one of the ship's OS2U Kingfisher planes into the air. The *Texas* continued closing on the island, but as dawn broke, it became evident that a heavy mist and low-lying clouds had obscured the battleship's targets ashore.

By 8:02 A.M. visibility had cleared enough to allow the spotter pilot to see some targets on the island, and Captain Baker gave the order to commence firing. After only five salvos, however, the *Texas* had to cease fire as increasing clouds and decreasing visibility made it impossible for the spotter to see the target or the impact of the 14-inch shells.[6]

Visibility continued to be problematic throughout the day, and the *Texas'* Kingfisher spotter plane was also periodically harassed by Japanese airplanes. During the day, the main battery fired 124 rounds of 14-inch high-capacity ammunition and destroyed a number of enemy artillery emplacements, bunkers, and caves. Firing ceased at

One of the seaplanes of the U.S.S. Texas.

5:05 P.M., and the *Texas* sailed to the night retirement area northwest of the enemy-held island.

On the following morning, Captain Baker had the crew at their air defense stations at 5:00 A.M. in anticipation of Japanese air attacks. At 6:21, as it was growing light enough to see, the aviation department catapulted one of the spotter planes into the air, and the crew prepared for another day of bombarding enemy positions on the island. At 7:00 A.M. the *Texas* fired the first salvo of the day, destroying a Japanese pillbox at a range of 10,200 yards. After pummeling enemy targets for an hour, the battleship ceased firing and launched a second spotter plane, while recovering the first. At 9:30 the *Texas* resumed her punishment of the island. The Japanese responded by firing anti-aircraft weapons at the Kingfisher spotter planes, which generally evaded the fire and were seldom hit.

Shortly after noon, Navy Underwater Demolitions Team (UDT) swimmers began their operations to clear the landing area of underwater obstacles. The *Texas* moved in toward the island until she was only two thousand yards from the beach, to provide close fire support for the UDT men.

As the *Texas* slowly steamed closer to the coast, a flight of U.S. Army Air Forces B-24 Liberators flew over and bombed the beach. The last plane in the flight was hit by Japanese anti-aircraft fire and emitted smoke as it flew out of sight, still defiantly firing its 50-caliber machineguns at the island. Shortly after the air attack, the Navy swimmers went in and placed explosives on underwater obstacles in the approaches to the invasion beaches.

Harold Long, a First Class Seaman on the *Texas*, watched the action from the main deck as the Navy swimmers placed their explosives then swam back out to be picked up by Higgins boats. Once all the frogmen were accounted for, all the underwater demolitions were exploded.[7]

The *Texas* continued with gunfire support missions until 6:40 P.M. The ship had expended 242 rounds of 14-inch ammunition and 439 rounds of 5-inch shells that day. Targets destroyed included two aircraft, a small ammunition dump, several anti-aircraft weapons, and numerous pillboxes.[8]

February 18 was largely a repeat of the previous day, with the main battery firing on targets visible to the Kingfisher spotter planes, while the secondary battery of 5-inch guns fired on targets located by spotters in the foremast. The bombardment routine was interrupted during the mid-morning, when one of the spotter planes was dispatched on a rescue mission to pick up a pilot who had to ditch his plane in the sea one hundred miles east of Mount Suribachi. After successfully locating and saving the pilot of a shot-down FM-2 Wildcat fighter, the Kingfisher observation plane returned to the *Texas*, proving once again the value and versatility of the old battleship and her crew.[9]

February 19, 1945, was D-Day for Iwo Jima. The *Texas* arrived at its fire support position approximately 4,200 yards off the southwestern tip of the island and opened fire with her main battery on pre-

The U.S.S. Texas *with Mount Suribachi in the background.*

arranged targets at 6:50 A.M. The hazy, misty weather of the previous two days gave way to clear skies, and the pilots in the Kingfisher spotter planes, as well as the spotters in the foremast, had unobstructed views of Iwo Jima Island and the battleship's targets there. The gun crews on the *Texas* opened fire with a vengeance, obliterating Japanese artillery pieces, pillboxes, and machineguns with devastating fire from 14-inch and 5-inch guns. At eight in the morning, the ship ceased firing while seventy-two carrier-based fighters and bombers made low-level strikes, dropping their deadly cargoes on the landing beaches and on the dominating Mount Suribachi, the highest point on the Island. Following on the heels of the first strike, an additional forty-eight fighters blasted the beaches and adjoining areas with napalm, rockets, and machinegun fire. As the naval aircraft attacked, the old battleship moved up to within 2,200 yards, or just over one nautical mile, of the shore. The *Texas* again opened fire on previously selected targets, taking advantage of this last opportunity to smother the Japanese opposition before the Marines landed. The ship stopped firing just minutes before the first wave of Marines hit the beach at

9:00. Moving up to within 2,000 yards of the shore, the crew of the *Texas* had a front-row seat to the amphibious assault.[10]

E.A. McCampbell was a radar operator on the main battery gun director. From his vantage point on the foremast he could see the beach clearly. "We were up shooting 14-inch shells over the Marines as they went up the bank," he remembered. "It was pretty rough. Not on us, it was on the Marines. We were shooting anti-personnel over their heads as they went up the bank. A lot of them didn't make it up the bank."[11]

During the invasion at Iwo Jima, Gunner's Mate Eneva Limerick manned a 20-millimeter gun on the port side, amidships. He recalled that on the day of the invasion, "we lowered our main battery guns right onto the shore and just blasted the entire area, trying to clear away where the landing took place. I just didn't think anything could live and stand that kind of punishment." To his surprise, however, he related "when we stopped firing we actually saw tanks, these old Japanese tanks, come lumbering down the hillside there to meet the landing craft and the Marines that were coming ashore. I couldn't believe that that could occur."[12]

Not all the Marines in the fleet stormed the beach that day. The battleship *Texas* had her own Marine detachment of eighty-five men, and many of them watched as their fellow Devil Dogs fought their way ashore. Marine PFC Ralph Fletcher had an unobstructed view of the landing at Iwo Jima from his position on Mount Eight, a 40-millimeter anti-aircraft gun on the port side. "The Marines came right in under our guns on those landing craft," he asserted. "I could see them; we were as close as a thousand yards. When a tank would get stopped, or when a guy got wounded or killed, you could usually tell which was which."[13]

At about 8:30 A.M. waves of troop-laden Landing Vehicles, Tracked, or LVTs, crossed the line of departure and began chugging toward the shore. After the seemingly endless passage to the island, the assault regiments from the 4th and 5th Marine Divisions stormed ashore from their LVTs at about five minutes after nine. As the Marines raced up the beach, their advance slowed to a walk as they sank into the powdery, loose, volcanic ash.

Even though the bombardment from the *Texas* and other ships and the aerial attacks from U.S. aircraft had destroyed many Japanese defenses and killed many Japanese soldiers, many more lay hiding in well-protected and camouflaged bunkers. As the U.S. Marines moved up the beach, the Japanese defenders came out of their pillboxes and caves and poured out a withering fire from rifles, automatic weapons, mortars, and artillery. The Marines continued advancing, but at a cost in blood and lives for every yard gained.

Small bands of intrepid Marines fought their way across the island from the landing beaches and reached the opposite side as early as 10:35 that morning, but the fight was just beginning. Japanese resistance increased, as did the Marine casualties, and Mount Suribachi, the hiding place for Japanese observers and many enemy guns, began receiving more attention from the ships providing gunfire support to the Marines.[14]

The crew of the *Texas* did their best to locate and eliminate the enemy as the Marines fought their way across the island. While seeking targets for the guns of the *Texas,* the crews of the spotter planes had a close up and personal view of the battle. The sights witnessed by some of the men stayed with them for the rest of their lives. Radio Operator Tom Koltuniak recalled, "I couldn't talk about it for about eight or ten years, and I had wild-ass dreams. But I'll bet that I saw five hundred Marines get killed. I mean that was, it was horrible. And you know from eight hundred, nine hundred feet," he pointed out, "it's not that far away. You're looking right down at it. It was a sad situation."[15]

Koltuniak's plane was also shot up, and the pilot had to crash-land the Kingfisher in the sea. He remembered, "We landed just off shore, maybe a mile or so. There was a picket boat that came to pick us up, and I stayed with it because I wanted to make damn sure that the IFF [Identify, Friend or Foe radio device] was blown. I just jumped off the plane [onto the boat], then they called on one of the nearby destroyers to just home in on it and get rid of it." He concluded: "They just blew it up."[16]

During their time at Iwo Jima, the threat of Japanese air attack caused a continuous level of anxiety for Captain Baker and his crew.

Manning the anti-aircraft guns continuously during the day meant the crew put in long hours during the battle, and meal service had to take into account the need to keep the men at their battle stations. The cooks prepared a good hot breakfast and served it to the crew at 4:00 A.M. so the sailors could be at their air defense stations at 5:00. The men then had a snack of coffee cake or other baked goods around 10:00, and later a dinner of "K" rations at noon, which the crew ate at their general quarters posts. The crew was released from general quarters an hour or so after sundown, at which time they had their supper, which was a hot, heavy meal. Then at midnight, the cooks served sandwiches and coffee to the men on watch. In this manner the crew remained adequately fed while providing maximum protection to the ship.[17]

One of the most inspiring events of the Iwo Jima battle, and an image that has come to represent American valor and sacrifice, occurred on February 23, when a group of Marines from the 2nd Battalion, 28th Marine Regiment raised the American flag at the top of Mount Suribachi. In actuality, there were two flag raisings, the first being a small, 28- by 54-inch flag, raised at 10:20 that morning. Shortly after the initial flag went up, another group of Marines replaced it with a larger flag, measuring 4 feet 8 inches by 8 feet, which could be clearly seen both ashore and by the ships in the area. The second flag raising was captured on film by photographer Joe Rosenthal, and the image has become immortalized as the Marine Corps War Memorial at Arlington National Cemetery in Virginia.

Pharmacist's Mate James Naismith watched the flag-raising on Mount Suribachi through the spotting scope of a 3-inch anti-aircraft gun on the deck of the *Texas*. The Marines were trying to get up the hill, struggling through the loose black ash, when a small Japanese tank appeared. It was so tiny it looked almost like a toy, and men on the ship could see the red fire coming out from the gun in front. The Marines nearest the tank crouched down, and as it neared them, they jumped up on the back of the tank. One of them thrust a hand grenade into the hatch of the tank, and the resulting explosion blew the treads of the tank away. Naismith and the other men watching from the ship laughed at the comical sight, not realizing until later how serious it had been.[18]

At Iwo Jima, Marine PFC Ralph Fletcher had an excellent view of the island from his 40-millimeter anti-aircraft gun. "One of the highlights of the whole trip to me was at Iwo Jima," he asserted. He remembered that the chaplain "came on the PA system and said, 'Attention all hands. Look toward Mount Suribachi.' We were only about one thousand yards off the island. So we looked, and sure enough you could see the flag go up over there on top of Mount Suribachi." Fletcher concluded: "that was a spine-tingling thing, and it's something I'll never forget."[19]

The fighting on Iwo Jima continued for weeks after the initial landing, and General Schmidt, commander of all the Marines in the battle, finally declared the island secured on March 26. While the battle continued to rage, however, the U.S. forces involved saw the first positive result of their efforts.

Ed Reichert was an officer in the Combat Information Center, or CIC, at Iwo Jima. "I remember the first B-29 that came in and landed there," he wrote. "It was a cripple; it was damaged in a raid over Japan. And that was the most rewarding thing, to know that we had accomplished something, to give those planes a place to land if they were damaged on the way back. They mostly came from Saipan. Iwo Jima was the stopping place," he explained, "only if they were damaged."[20]

The first B-29 landed at Iwo Jima on March 4, 1945, while the Marines and Japanese battled over possession of the airfield, and the Marines occupied only one end of the landing strip. The Japanese held the other end. Luckily the American bomber came to rest on the Marine end. By the end of major hostilities on the island on March 26, thirty-six crippled B-29 Superfortress bombers had made emergency landings on Iwo Jima. By the end of the war a total of 2,251 American bombers carrying 24,761 crewmen had landed on the island. The majority of these men would have been lost at sea if the emergency landing strip at Iwo Jima were not available.[21]

With other combat actions looming before them, the crew of the *Texas* had to leave Iwo Jima before the Marines ashore ultimately defeated the Japanese foe, bringing the United States one step closer to the final victory. As the *Texas* departed the island on March 8, her crew could take pride in the fact that they had contributed immeasurably to the success of American arms and that that their efforts had lessened the toll of American lives in this horrific conflict. At the conclusion of the fight, Admiral Chester Nimitz said of the battle, "Among the Americans who served on Iwo Island uncommon valor was a common virtue." The men of the *Texas* agreed.

CHAPTER TEN

The Last Battle— The U.S.S. *Texas* at Okinawa

The *Texas* departed from the waters of Iwo Jima on March 7 and headed for the Caroline Islands for replenishment, repairs, and some well-earned recreation for the crew. At the island of Mog-Mog the men could go ashore for a few hours and lie around in the sun, swim, or play softball. In an effort to make the swimming safer, Navy Construction Battalion sailors, known as Seabees, had placed netting in the water around the beach to keep the sharks away. When sailors reported to the island, they received three cans of warm beer, or three bottles of warm Coca-Cola. Many of the sailors who didn't care for the uncooled beer sold it to others who were less discriminating.[1] While the men certainly enjoyed the carefree days at Mog-Mog, they all knew that additional battles, and perhaps tougher ones, lay ahead.

After taking on supplies and ammunition, the *Texas*, accompanied by the *Tennessee*, left the Ulithi lagoon on March 21 and steamed for the Japanese island of Okinawa. On the 24th the ship met up with others of the fire support unit, and by 7:00 A.M. on March 25 the *Texas* was in her assigned position, to protect smaller ships conducting minesweeping operations. Shortly after noon the *Texas* ceased covering the minesweepers, and at 2:28 P.M. Captain Baker gave the

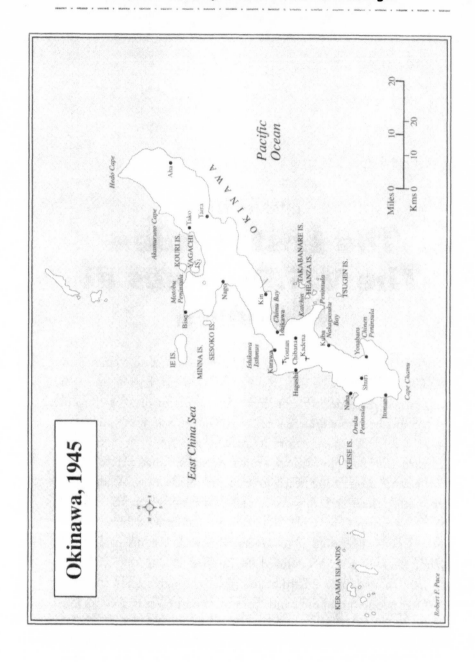

Okinawa, 1945

Robert F. Pace

order to commence fire, and the old dreadnought once again began firing its main battery in a scheduled bombardment of Japanese shore installations. After firing for about two hours, the *Texas* left the area, and steamed toward a retirement area for the night.[2]

The next several days were a repetition of the same activity, shelling the Japanese positions on Okinawa during the day, and just before dusk breaking away from the action to sail to a night retirement area. Often the *Texas* provided support and protection to the minesweepers while they attempted to clear the approaches to the invasion beaches, and at times the ship became a floating gas station, as destroyers and smaller vessels received fuel from the cavernous oil bunkers of the battleship.

The bombardment routine was interrupted on the afternoon of March 29, when lookouts on the *Texas* spotted a man in the water some five hundred yards off the starboard bow.[3] Closer inspection through the lookout's binoculars revealed that the man was struggling to stay afloat. He was not wearing a blue Navy life jacket, or the yellow Mae West life preserver issued to air crewmen. The lookout reported to the bridge that the man in the water appeared to be Japanese. Captain Baker ordered a crew of boatswain's mates to arm themselves with rifles, launch a boat, and recover the Japanese. Before the crew departed, he cautioned them to take no chances with the man. If he resisted, Captain Baker instructed the men, "Shoot him."

The rescue crew launched a whaleboat and motored over to the swimming man and prepared to bring him aboard the boat. As the sailors reached for him, he tried to pull a revolver out of his holster, but one of the boatswain's mates was ready and struck him in the face with the butt of a Springfield rifle. The Japanese dropped his revolver into the sea and offered no further resistance.

When the boat and crew returned to the *Texas*, they pulled up on the port side amidships, just aft of mount eight, a 40-millimeter gun adjacent to the galley. Crewmen on the ship dropped a line over the side, and the boat crew tied the rope around the prisoner. The deck gang pulled him up to the top of the blister, where Marines from the ship's detachment waited to take him into custody. While he was

A Japanese pilot captured by the crew of the Texas.

standing on the port blister, the Marines cut his clothing off to make sure he wasn't hiding a grenade or other weapon.

After giving him a pair of Navy dungarees, the Marines took the prisoner to sick bay where a corpsman examined him. The prisoner, a Japanese Navy petty officer, was a muscular man, though short, with a well-defined physique. He had been in the water for several hours, but was in good health. He had been a pilot of a kamikaze plane, but had either been shot down or decided against crashing his plane into an American ship. As none of the crew of the *Texas* spoke Japanese, Captain Baker held the prisoner in the brig for a time, and then transferred him to another ship for interrogation by intelligence specialists.[4]

April 1, 1945, was both April Fool's Day and Easter Sunday. It was also the day that leathernecks of the 1st and 6th Marine Divisions and soldiers of the 7th and 96th Infantry Divisions invaded the Japanese Island of Okinawa. At six minutes after four in the morning Admiral Richmond Kelly Turner, commander of all the amphibious forces, gave the traditional order, "Land the Landing Force." As the soldiers and Marines began the process of disembarking from their troop transports and clambering down into the landing craft, the ships of the fire support units moved into position. The *Texas* and several other ships steamed to the southeastern side of the island, and at 6:45 A.M. Captain Baker gave the order for the main battery to commence firing. The job of the old dreadnought this time was to trick the Japanese defenders into believing that the amphibious attack would take place on the southeastern beaches, where elements of the 2nd Marine Division were to fake a landing while the actual assault occurred on the other side of the island.[5]

As the *Texas* bombarded the coast, the real landing took place at 8:30 A.M., and the landing craft for the feint invasion zoomed in toward the beach, then turned around and headed back out to sea. The ruse was successful and pinned down many Japanese troops that otherwise could have attacked the soldiers and Marines actually coming ashore across the island. For the remainder of the day the *Texas* continued with the scheduled bombardment, interspersed with occasional calls for fire from units ashore.

The naval bombardment of the island was impressive to Americans and Japanese alike. A Japanese officer who witnessed it wrote in his diary that the massive barrage was "a scene of unsurpassed grandeur."[6] Ernie Pyle, probably the greatest correspondent of that entire terrible war, accompanied the Marines during the invasion and was on a small ship near the beaches during some of the bombardment. He wrote that the shelling "set up vibrations in the air—a sort of flutter—which pained and pounded the ears as though with invisible drumsticks."[7] The massive 14-inch shells of the *Texas'* guns contributed to the devastation ashore, which saved the lives of many Americans fighting their way across the beach.

By this time in the war, April 1945, surface ships of the Japanese Navy were no longer a serious threat to American forces. The major menace was in the form of Japanese airplanes, especially suicide pilots, or kamikazes. During the Iwo Jima Campaign, Japanese airplanes launched numerous attacks on U.S. ships, but it was at Okinawa that the kamikazes planes came in droves in an attempt to obliterate American shipping. Captain Baker responded to the threat by taking extreme measures. He kept his crew at their anti-aircraft battle stations for fifty days straight. All day and all night, the men remained at their battle stations, eating and sleeping right beside their weapons.

Crewmember Eneva Limerick remembered the time vividly. "Okinawa was a real endurance contest. At that time my battle station had changed to sky aft. I was an aircraft spotter up in the top of the mainmast. And we stayed there for fifty-two days without coming down." Describing some of the more delicate problems with constant duty, he recalled, "anything we had to do, we did in a bucket and lowered it down on a rope and had it thrown overboard. We ate K-rations. Once every couple of days they allowed some of the crew to come down and get a hot meal. Otherwise it was all K-rations."[8]

During the early morning of April 12 the men of the *Texas* had their closest call, when a determined Japanese suicide pilot made an attempt to crash his plane into the battleship. John Monsies was a crewman on a 3-inch anti-aircraft gun and witnessed the attack.

> One day we had a kamikaze plane coming on the starboard side and we start shooting and I was pointer and pulling the trigger. This kamikaze plane kept coming lower and lower until it got about forty, fifty feet above the water. It kept coming, kept coming. We kept shooting, and there was pieces of that plane coming off. He kept coming anyway. And right behind him was a plane, I don't know if it was a Navy plane, or a Marine Corps plane, or Army. And that plane kept right on his tail. And I just kept [thinking], "I wish that guy would just pull up, because we might hit him." And I know I can remember I was aiming low as I could, and he kept following. He followed that plane within four or five hundred feet from the ship.
>
> And I don't know who hit the [Japanese] plane, but the plane went down and splashed water all over us. But, thank God, we did not hit that [American] plane. And the plane went up over our mast, and he just tipped his wings a few times. That still bothers me. That was the bravest thing I ever saw.[9]

The Mitsubishi G4M1 twin-engine "Betty" bomber crashed in flames only fifty yards off the starboard quarter.[10]

A second determined kamikaze pilot attempted to destroy himself and the *Texas* a few days later, on April 16. The plane, identified as a Nakajima B5N "Kate," came flying in from astern through a smoke screen. Anti-aircraft gunners on the *Texas* and several other ships opened fire on the plane, as Captain Baker turned his ship to present the port beam to the enemy plane, so that all of the gunners on the port side could bring their anti-aircraft guns to bear on the target. The maneuver was successful, as the plane crashed into the water 1,800 yards off the port beam.[11]

During the Okinawa Campaign, each ship in the fleet took turns firing illumination shells at night to light up the front lines for the ground troops ashore and to lessen the chances of a sneak Japanese attack at night. When it was the turn of the *Texas*, the gunners fired the star-shells from the 3-inch guns. They kept the illumination up all night long, and as one parachute flare burned out, the gunners fired another one. The sharp, high-pitched crack of the 3-inch gun precluded any sleep for any of the men on deck. Just when a man got drowsy enough to drop off to sleep, the gunners fired another star-shell, all through the night.[12]

The ships of the Pacific Fleet received word on April 15 that the man who had led the United States since 1933, in peace and in war, President Franklin Delano Roosevelt, had died. That morning the *Texas* was at Okinawa, firing in support of the troops ashore, when abruptly all of the firing stopped, and an eerie silence descended on the ships arrayed around the island. Captain Baker came on the ship's intercom and announced to the crew that word had just been received that President Roosevelt had died, and the ships of the fleet would observe a brief period of silence. Many of the crewmembers felt lost and worried, as President Roosevelt had served for the last twelve years, and he was the only president they had known or could remember. What would they do without him? How could they live, and win, without the leadership of the man they had known and trusted and admired for so long? Was the unknown vice president, Harry Truman up to the job?[13]

The fighting ashore continued day after day, as the Marine and Army ground-pounders slogged their way across the island, rooting out the Japanese defenders. Each day brought additional Japanese aerial attacks on the fleet, and the toll of damaged or sunk U.S. ships increased daily. The crew of the *Texas* fired at numerous enemy planes and watched in frustrated anger as the fanatical Japanese plunged their planes into nearby American ships.

The crew of the *Texas* watched as the destroyer *Zellars* shot down two suicide planes, only to be hit by a third. Minutes later another kamikaze slammed into the battleship *Tennessee*. During the weeks at Okinawa, the *Texas* crewmen anxiously scanned the skies and blazed away at enemy airplanes so often that it became almost routine. An anxious dread came over many of the men, as they saw ship after ship take hits from enemy aircraft.

During the Okinawa Campaign the OS2U Kingfisher spotter planes of the *Texas* were constantly in the air, seeking enemy targets to destroy. While the pilot flew the plane and looked for the enemy, the radio operator in the rear seat also scanned the area for likely targets and often put his machineguns to good use. Tom Koltuniak was a radio operator in the aviation department and flew in the back seat of the OS2U over Iwo Jima. "I shot a Japanese horse, and I shot up a Japanese truck, and I shot up a hill where there was an ammunition dump," he asserted. "It blew up like you wouldn't believe. I remember just hitting that hill because there was a guy on a motorcycle heading for it. But I kept on shooting and all of a sudden that hill just went to hell. It went into a bunker or an ammunition dump or whatever."[14]

In addition to spotting the gunfire of the main batteries, the ship's planes also carried out photographic missions and occasionally engaged in more offensive measures, such as strafing small Japanese boats approaching U.S. ships. Not all of the Kingfisher spotter planes escaped unscathed from their encounters with the enemy. On April 27 one of the OS2Us was hit by anti-aircraft fire, and a shell fragment struck radio operator H.D. "Red" Jahnke in the leg, so he could not catch the hook as the plane landed in the water beside the battleship.

The pilot, Ensign Thompson, jumped out and tried to catch the hook, but was unable to grab it as his plane began to drift away from the ship. The battle-damaged pontoon began filling with water, and Ensign Thompson just barely had time to get the radio operator out of the damaged aircraft before the plane flipped over and sank.[15]

One reason why the pilot missed the hook was because the pilot landed on the wrong side of the *Texas*, downwind from the bulky battleship. The correct way was to land upwind so the breeze blows the plane to the ship, rather than away from it. Once the crew fished the two aviators out of the sea, Captain Baker summoned the pilot to the bridge.

"You are a Naval officer, and you don't know port from starboard?" Captain Baker asked the pilot. Ensign Thompson replied, "I thought I did pretty good to get back on either side."[16]

While the war against the Japanese in the Pacific was grinding onward, the war in Europe against Germany reached its victorious climax. As U.S. and British forces entered Germany from the west, the Red Army of the Soviet Union invaded Germany from the east, and the Allies ultimately crushed all German resistance. Representatives of the German Army agreed to surrender, and newly-installed President Harry Truman declared May 8, 1945, as "V-E Day," for Victory in Europe. On that day at noon all the ships that could bring a gun to bear on Okinawa fired a full salvo at pre-selected targets ashore.[17]

Victory in Europe had been achieved, but victory against Japan was still elusive, and the fighting continued. Day after day the *Texas* fired her 14-inch main battery and 5-inch secondary battery at enemy targets, churning up the landscape and sending numerous Japanese soldiers to perdition, while watching out for the ever-present kamikaze menace. Although the fighting on Okinawa continued through June, the old battleship finally departed the embattled island's waters on May 14 and headed for Leyte Gulf, in the Philippine Islands, arriving there three days later. The vessel remained in Philippine waters for the next two months, undergoing maintenance, repair, and anti-aircraft training in anticipation of the next mission, whatever that might be.[18]

During the seven weeks the ship actively participated in the Okinawa operation, the *Texas* expended 2,019 rounds from the main battery of 14-inch guns, and 2,643 rounds from the secondary battery of 5-inch guns.[19] The seasoned veteran gunners on the *Texas* provided valuable assistance to the troops ashore, firing in support of the 1st and 6th Marine Divisions, as well as soldiers of the 7th, 27th, 77th and 96th Infantry Divisions of the Army. As in previous campaigns and battles, the aging dreadnought and her skillful and valiant crew contributed significantly to the final victory at Okinawa.

After the conclusion of the brutal and bloody campaign, the U.S. Naval, Marine, and Army forces involved breathed a collective sigh of relief and then began preparing for the next battle—the invasion of the home islands of Japan itself. The deadly and ever-increasing threat from Japanese suicide planes was manifestly evident to the men of the *Texas* and the fleet in general. As the older ships of the battle line girded themselves for the coming invasion of Japan, Navy commanders recommended changes and improvements to the *Texas*.

Captain Baker wrote in his after-action report that "the anti-aircraft battery as installed aboard is considered to be inadequate for the present assignments of this vessel."[20] The ship's 5-inch guns could only be used for surface bombardment and could not be brought to bear on aircraft. The 3-inch guns may have been adequate anti-aircraft protection in 1916, when they were first installed, but were obsolete by 1945.

Admiral P.K. Fischler, commander of Battleship Division Five, echoed Captain Baker's sentiments. Admiral Fischler recommended that the Navy remove one of the 14-inch turrets from the *Texas*, as well as all the 5-inch/51-caliber guns, and the 3-inch antiaircraft guns. In their place the *Texas* should have installed a battery of modern 5-inch/38-caliber dual-purpose guns, such as those placed on the *Iowa* class battleships, the newest in the fleet. While the recommended changes certainly would have better protected the *Texas*, the Navy did not act on Admiral Fischler's suggestions.[21]

CHAPTER ELEVEN

The End of the War Comes to the *Texas*

By August 1945 the battleship *Texas* and her valiant crew had served the United States proudly and faithfully during forty-four months of combat. From the beginning of the war, when the ship was at Casco Bay, Maine, through convoy duties, to firing in support of amphibious invasions, the old dreadnought and the men who sailed on her served with distinction.

But the biggest battle remained—the invasion of Japan—the final battle that would end the war. The United States Navy, Marine Corps, and Army knew the toughest campaign of the war would be for the conquest of the home islands of Japan, and the *Texas* would once again be in the forefront of the fighting. Too slow to accompany the fast carriers, the *Texas* had proved worthy as a gunfire support platform, a duty the vessel would perform in the Invasion of Japan, where she would once again be a target for numerous suicide planes. But the conclusive final battle was not to be.

In August 1945 the battleship *Texas* was with the fleet at Leyte Gulf in the Philippines when the inconceivable happened—Japan surrendered. The killing was over. The dying was over. The war was over. The men dared to hope, to believe, that they would live and not die in battle.

On Friday evening, August 10, the crew had finished their supper and the officers and men were on the forecastle, waiting for the evening movie to begin. While it was growing dark enough to show the film, the ship's orchestra began to play. Finally Captain Baker made his way to his chair, the screen was moved into place, and the movie began. But then Lieutenant Fitzgerald, the officer of the watch, came on the ship's public address system, and called out "Attention all hands." The movie stopped, and the boisterous sailors became quiet. Then Lieutenant Fitzgerald announced, "Japan has notified the Allies that she is willing to accept the terms of the Potsdam conference." For just a moment the great ship was silent, and then a sustained roar rocked her from one end to the other, as the men expressed their delight in the almost incomprehensible news.

It was a night that those who experienced it would remember forever. Watertender W.C. Black and some of his buddies were lying on a blanket on the forecastle near the port anchor chain watching the movie when he heard of the surrender. The rest of the night he and his friends celebrated by staying up all night, shooting craps, playing cards, and telling lies to each other.

Al Alexander remembered many of the other ships in the harbor firing off their anti-aircraft guns into the sky during the night of exuberance. The next morning the wooden deck of the *Texas* was littered with bits of steel shrapnel from the stray celebratory shots.[1]

Eneva Limerick remembered the night well. "We were in Leyte Gulf that night, and there was the greatest fireworks display of the boats and ships in Leyte Gulf. It looked like the Fourth of July times a thousand. Everybody was just firing guns up in the air. Tracers just completely filled the sky." Some men retrieved cans of beer they had kept hidden for weeks or months to celebrate the joyous occasion.

The most crowded Buglemaster Will John Eddleman ever saw the main deck was after the announcement of the surrender of Japan. The last cell of the brig contained 5-gallon cans of 200 proof medicinal alcohol. Someone broke into the brig and stole the alcohol and made a large beverage of the alcohol and fruit juice. Eddleman did not have any of the juice, but many of the sailors did, and it took only a cup or two to knock them out.[2]

The celebration of the end of the war was tempered somewhat the following week. On Friday, August 17, Capt. Charles A. Baker, the man who had led the *Texas* and her crew through eighteen months of training, trial, and combat, turned command of the ship over to his replacement, Capt. Gerald Schetky. In a brief ceremony on the main deck, Captain Baker addressed his crew one last time.

Well men this is it. This is what we have been working for since the attack on Pearl Harbor. I know how you men feel, and this is your night to howl.

I know at times I have given some of you men hell, and you know that, but every thing I have done to you, or for you, was for the good of the ship.

The TEXAS has been like a home to me, and I am truly proud of the men who made her that way. The people back home say the Navy is made of iron, but really and truly it is you men. The men of the TEXAS are made of iron. My heart has been with and will remain with the TEXAS and you men.

You know that the men of the fleet just marvel how we stayed at General Quarters for some fifty days. That is why I think we are here today. We were always ready for anything that should come up. Some ships got theirs while they were at chow, or at some other activity. We have heard other ships going into evening alert, but we were always there and ready.

I was kind of sorry to receive my orders this morning, and that I would have to leave you before the war was over, but now that it has happened I can always say that we saw it through together, and to the end! And we've been through a lot, and have seen some blood and thunder together.

I again say that the ship is yours tonight, and you can do all the yelling and howling you want to.

After the conclusion of hostilities the *Texas*, along with many other ships of the fleet, transported American servicemen back to the United States in a massive undertaking called Operation Magic Carpet. The first men returned home by the *Texas* was a group of U.S. prisoners of war liberated from Japan. Smaller ships brought the rescued former prisoners to the *Texas* for transport back to the states. Most of the men were badly emaciated and were little more than walking skeletons. The doctors and corpsmen of the *Texas* gave physical exams to all of the men and gave them shots to combat the various diseases from which the men suffered. Many of the men were admitted into sickbay, and the overflow patients were placed in bunks nearest sickbay. The crew tried their best to feed the starved men, to put some meat on their bones and restore them to a semblance of good health. The *Texas* sailed from Okinawa to Pearl Harbor and then on to San Pedro Harbor in Los Angeles, arriving there on October 15. At San Pedro the precious cargo of liberated American prisoners went ashore to waiting ambulances and hospital personnel.[3]

At noon on October 30 the *Texas* stood out from Long Beach, California, steaming for Pearl Harbor where she arrived on November 5. After hurriedly embarking almost 1,500 servicemen as passengers, the *Texas* once again got under way on November 6, headed for San Francisco. The ship arrived there on November 13 and departed on the 18th, taking a load of 670 fresh troops to Pearl Harbor. Pulling into Pearl on November 24, the *Texas* disembarked her passengers and on the following day brought aboard 1,415 men for transportation to San Diego, where she arrived on December 4. After safely delivering the returning servicemen, the *Texas* steamed for Terminal Island at Long Beach, where the vessel entered dry dock for post-voyage repairs. After a rushed repair job, the old battleship once again got underway and made for Pearl Harbor on December 12. The crew anxiously wondered if they could make it back home to the states for Christmas.[4]

Arriving at Pearl Harbor on the afternoon of December 18, the firemen in the boiler rooms of the *Texas* kept the ship's steam up, an unusual occurrence for a capital ship mooring in a harbor. Just as anxious to get home as the men of the *Texas* were 110 officers and 1305 enlisted men waiting on the pier. The passengers quickly came aboard, and the battleship was underway once again after spending less than three hours in port. The race was on to get home for Christmas.[5]

At 10:42 on the morning of Christmas Eve 1945 the *Texas* docked at the Navy Pier, in San Diego, and disembarked the last load of passengers for Operation Magic Carpet, after bringing home a total of more than five thousand U.S. servicemen. The ship had been constantly at sea and on the move and had no Christmas trees or decorations of any kind. Pharmacist's Mate James Naismith took up a collection from his shipmates, and he and a buddy went to San Diego in search of some Christmas decorations. They could find nothing to buy anyplace and finally went into a five and ten-cent store that had a Christmas display in the window.

The young sailor said to the clerk, "Look, you don't have any Christmas trees or decorations left and we need one for the ship. We don't have any Christmas decorations at all." The young lady replied, "I'm sorry, but I can't sell you anything, we don't have anything to sell you." Naismith responded, "But you have a tree in the window." The clerk replied, "I can't sell you that, it's a display item." Naismith pleaded, "Well, look, we just got in and we have no decorations at all. Most of the people on board the ship have been there all during the war." The lady softened, but said, "Well, I feel very sorry for you, but let me get the manager."

Naismith then repeated his story to the manager, who exclaimed, "Oh, of course you can have the tree." The manager then went to the window and retrieved the tree and many extra ornaments for the sailors. Naismith then asked, "Well, how much do we owe you? We have twenty dollars here, we can pay you for this." The manager replied, "You don't owe me a thing." Naismith took the tree and decorations back to the ship, and adorned the sickbay with the tree, tinsel, and ornaments for a festive Christmas Eve.[6]

Following the celebration of Christmas in California, the *Texas* once again put to sea and made its last trip through the Panama

Canal, headed to the East Coast. After arriving in Norfolk on February 13, the crew prepared to deactivate the great ship. Over the next several weeks the sailors removed consumable items, weapons, and anything that could be used on other, active duty, ships. In June 1946 the Navy towed the *Texas* to Baltimore, Maryland, where the ship was stored with other mothballed relics of the past war. Her service life was over, and the battlewagon's only future appeared to be a date with the scrap yard. Like so many other proud ships, the *Texas*, no longer needed to protect our country, was to be cut up and sold for scrap.

CHAPTER TWELVE

Rebirth of the *Texas*— A New Role for an Old Ship

But life for the *Texas* was not over.

For several months the old battleship languished at her berth while leaders within the United States Navy decided what to do with the numerous aging ships no longer needed for the defense of our country. The Navy decided to scrap some half-dozen old battleships, unless the states for which they were named wanted to take them as war memorials. When the Navy contacted the political leaders in the Lone Star State, the Texans jumped at the chance to bring the battleship back to her namesake state. The only catch was that the state must come up with at least $225,000.00 to pay the cost of towing the ship from the East Coast and preparing an adequate place to moor and display the vessel.

On April 17, 1947, the Texas Legislature passed a bill creating the Commission of Control for the Battleship *Texas*, as the first step in bringing the battleship to her new home. The commission consisted of nine people appointed by the governor, and it was the duty of the commission to raise the money to bring the ship to Texas and then to maintain and operate the battleship "as a permanent memorial for the purpose of commemorating the heroic participation of the State of

The way the Texas *looks today.*

Texas in the prosecution and victory of the Second World War." Gov. Buford Jester appointed Lloyd Gregory, managing editor of the Houston *Post*, chairman of the commission. Gregory and the other members began a fund drive to raise money for the ship.[1]

During the next several months the Battleship *Texas* Commission sent out appeals to the public for funds to bring the *Texas* home. Articles in various papers and numerous radio programs kept the old battleship in the headlines, and a short film clip was shown in movie theatres throughout the state. Public schools, American Legion posts, and Veterans of Foreign Wars chapters all pitched in to raise funds for the *Texas*, and their efforts were crowned with success when the old warship made its way through Galveston Bay and up the Houston Ship Channel to berth at the San Jacinto Battleground State Park, near Houston. The site for the new home of the *Texas*, as determined by the State Legislature, was a slip along the Houston Ship Channel, at the San Jacinto Battleground State Park. San Jacinto was the site where, on April 21, 1836, General Sam Houston defeated the Mexican Army of Gen. Antonio Lopez de Santa Anna, securing the independence of Texas from Mexico.

Wednesday, April 21, 1948, was a big day in the career of the *Texas*, and a big day for all those who worked to bring the ship to her home state. In an impressive ceremony held on the main deck of the battleship, Assistant Secretary of the Navy Mark Andrews, a native of Houston, formally presented the ship to Gov. Buford Jester.

Among the notables who participated in the ceremony were Fleet Admiral Chester W. Nimitz, former *Texas* chaplain Lt. Commander C.L. Moody, and Capt. Charles A. Baker, skipper of the *Texas* during its most active period. Captain Baker assumed command of the battleship on the ship's last day in the service of the United States, and he formally decommissioned the ship. After the conclusion of the ceremony, the ship was opened to the public, and the *Texas* began a new career as a museum and war memorial.[2]

The Battleship *Texas* Commission, chaired by Lloyd Gregory, hired a small caretaker staff, consisting of only three men during the early years. The Texas Legislature did not provide any funding for the operation of the ship, and the only money available for maintenance and repair came from admission fees charged to the visiting public. It was never enough. Maintaining a large and complicated structure is expensive and takes a great deal of time and effort. While an active-duty ship, the *Texas* had many hundreds of men to work on the vessel, but as an under-funded memorial, only a handful of staff serviced the battlewagon. Over the years, the ship suffered from lack of adequate maintenance and from the harsh climate and corrosive waters of the Houston Ship Channel. The *Texas* began to decline.

By 1968, the wooden main deck of the ship was so rotted that rainwater was leaking through the deck into the interior of the ship and pooling in various compartments of the vessel. The Battleship *Texas* Commission found that replacing the decayed deck timbers with teak wood was prohibitively expensive, so the Commission decided to remove the wooden deck and replace it with concrete. While cosmetically pleasing for a few years, the concrete soon cracked, and rainwater continued to leak through the main deck into spaces below.

In 1971, three local charitable institutions, the Brown Foundation, the Moody Foundation, and the Houston Endowment, together contributed $50,000.00 to the ship to enable the Battleship _Texas_ Commission to sandblast and paint the hull for the first time in twenty-three years. This much-needed maintenance project vastly improved the looks of the ship, but the hard-pressed maintenance staff was fighting a losing battle against the effects of time, corrosion, weather, and inadequate funding.

By 1983, several members of the Texas Legislature had grown dissatisfied with the way the Battleship _Texas_ Commission was handling the operations of the battleship memorial, and the Legislature abolished the Commission effective August 31, 1983. On the following day, September 1, the Texas Parks & Wildlife Department (TPWD) assumed operational control of the ship. TPWD already had responsibility for the park in which the battleship was moored and the nearby San Jacinto Monument.

One of the first actions of the TPWD was to hire a firm of naval architects to survey the ship in order to assess the deterioration and make recommendations as to what actions should be taken to preserve the old battlewagon. What they found was discouraging. The ship's watertight integrity was badly compromised, the hull was open to the sea in many places, and many compartments were full of standing rain water. The architects determined that the ship needed to go to dry dock for major repairs to the hull and to keep rain water from coming through the porous concrete deck.[3]

In 1986 the State of Texas celebrated its Sesquicentennial, or 150th anniversary. As a part of that celebration, the state legislature determined to embark upon a massive restoration project for the old battleship. On January 1, the Battleship _Texas_ Advisory Board, a new organization created to secure funding for the ship, began a campaign to raise ten million dollars for repairs and restoration.

While some raised money, others raised dust—or busted rust. In 1985, a number of volunteers began coming out to the ship to assist in the repair and restoration process. There were primarily three groups of volunteers: from the Exxon Refinery in Baytown, Houston Lighting and Power Company, and from the Baytown Fire Department. The three volunteer groups ultimately decided to consolidate, and in 1986 the combined volunteers elected Bernard Olive, with the Baytown Fire Department group, as the leader of the newly formed First Texas Volunteers (BB-35). This group provided dozens of volunteers who donated hundreds of hours toward rehabilitating the old warship.[4]

Finally in December 1988 the *Texas* was ready to leave the berth at San Jacinto and move to a dry dock at the Todd Shipyard at Galveston. The Battleship *Texas* Advisory Board helped raise money for the effort, working with public schools, charitable institutions, and large corporations. The U.S. Navy kicked in several million dollars, while the Texas Legislature appropriated additional millions for the restoration project.

On December 13, 1988, tugboats arrived at the berth of the *Texas* and, after several hours of effort, finally freed the ship from the mud in which it had been resting for forty years. The trip down the Houston Ship Channel to Galveston Bay and the Todd Shipyard took only a few hours, and the *Texas* spent the next year high and dry in the dock as yard workers engaged in massive repairs to the antiquated warship.

During the lengthy repair period, yard workers sand-blasted the decades-old paint from not only the hull but also the superstructure of the ship and replaced tons of rusted metal from the hull. Inside the ship, welders and fabricators replaced weakened structural beams and numerous rusted-out deck plates. Topside, workers removed the cement from the main deck and replaced it with wooden beams, just as it had been during her Navy days.

While Todd Shipyard worked on the *Texas*, state park officials began planning the continued restoration and historical interpretation of the ship. Park staff decided that the vessel should look as it did in March 1945, the period between the battles of Iwo Jima and Okinawa. While the ship was yet in the dock, state employees located and acquired from the U.S. Navy many objects to be used in the restoration of the ship, especially anti-aircraft guns. At the end of World War II, the Navy removed most of the anti-aircraft weapons, leaving the main deck empty. Bringing back the guns, especially the

The battleship Texas *in May 1945.*

40-millimeter quad mounts, to the main deck made the ship more closely resemble its late-war appearance.

After spending fourteen months in dry dock at Galveston, on February 24, 1990, tugboats moved the *Texas* from Todd Shipyard to a repair facility on Green's Bayou, just about four miles from the newly-renovated berth at San Jacinto. On July 26, 1990, the *Texas* returned to the San Jacinto Battleground State Historic Site. After additional work on the ship lasting about a month, she was once again opened to the public.[5]

Today the *Texas* rests quietly at berth in the San Jacinto State Park along the oak-covered shores of the Houston Ship Channel. The Battleship *Texas* is one of the most important historic navy ships in the world. This floating museum is the only ship of any type remaining in the United States that actively served in World War I and the only battleship remaining from any country that served in that war. In addition to being a military museum, the ship is also an engineering museum, being designated a National Historic Mechanical Engineering Landmark by the American Society of Mechanical Engineers in 1975. The vessel's historic status is further confirmed by its designation as a National Historic Landmark by the National Park Service in 1977.

In addition to the small but dedicated staff of state employees, the *Texas* is well served by the hard-working members of the First Texas Volunteers (BB-35). These men and women continue the on-going restoration process of the ship, serve as docents or tour guides and provide manpower for special events such as reunions of the crew of the *Texas*. Early into the 21st century, the First Texas Volunteers (BB-35) numbered over seventy-five members, who put in thousands of hours annually on the ship.

The Battleship *Texas* is a treasure of profound significance. Those who visit the ship cannot help being impressed, and all benefit from the experience. This historic vessel, which served from the days of American imperialism to the atomic age, is truly a fitting memorial to all those who have served and protected our great country.

Appendix A

Commanding Officers of the U.S.S. *Texas*

Name	Dates of Command		Length of Command
Albert W. Grant	March 12, 1914	June 10, 1915	456 days
John Hood	June 10, 1915	August 14, 1916	432 days
Victor Blue	August 14, 1916	December 31, 1918	870 days
Nathan C. Twining	December 31, 1918	July 17, 1919	199 days
Frank H. Schofield	July 17, 1919	June 17, 1921	702 days
Edward S. Kellog	June 17, 1921	July 6, 1922	385 days
Andre M. Proctor	July 6, 1922	May 22 1924	687 days
Ivan C. Wettengel	May 22, 1924	September 28, 1925	495 days
Charles A. Blakely	September 28, 1925	June 2, 1926	248 days
Zeno E. Biggs	June 2, 1926	January 4, 1928	582 days
Joseph R. Defrees	January 4, 1928	July 9, 1929	553 days
Adolphus Andrews	July 9, 1929	May 13, 1931	674 days
Julius C. Townsend	May 13, 1931	June 17, 1933	767 days
Lamar R. Leahy	June 17, 1933	April 15, 1935	668 days
Sherwood A. Taffinder	April 15, 1935	November 21, 1936	587 days
Fred Fremont Rogers	November 21, 1936	June 1, 1938	558 days
Robert R. M. Emmer	June 1, 1938	May 31, 1940	731 days
Clarence N. Hinkamp	May 31, 1940	August 2, 1941	429 days
Lewis W. Comstock	August 2, 1941	September 28, 1942	423 days
William E. Hennigar	September 28, 1942	October 3, 1942	6 days
Lawrence Wild	October 3, 1942	October 14, 1942	12 days
William E. Hennigar	October 14, 1942	October 17, 1942	4 days
Roy Pfaff	October 17, 1942	March 10, 1944	511 days
Charles A. Baker	March 10, 1944	August 17, 1945	526 days
Gerald L. Schetky	August 17, 1945	July 3, 1946	321 days
Robert N. Downes	July 3, 1946	March 6, 1947	247 days
James R. Bagshaw	March 6, 1947	April 7, 1947	33 days
Samuel J. McKee	April 7, 1947	July 31, 1947	116 days
Jack Steward	July 31, 1947	April 21, 1948	266 days
Charles A. Baker	April 21, 1948	April 21, 1948	1 day

Appendix B

Casualties of June 25, 1944

Killed in Action

Christiansen, Christen Norman, Quartermaster 3rd Class, of Brooklyn, New York. Helmsman.

Wounded in Action

Navigation Bridge

Anderson, Harvey Douglas. Quartermaster 3rd Class.
Apgar, William Louis. Yeoman First Class.
Foyle, Andrew Nelson. Seaman 1st Class.
Quigley, Henry Joseph. Seaman 2nd Class.
Saul, Emil Fred. Seaman 2nd Class.
Umholtz, Robert Leroy. Yeoman First Class.

Armored Conning Tower

Derickson, Richard Barnett. Lieutenant Commander.
Jordan, Kenneth Glenn. Seaman 1st Class.
Letourneau, Edward George. Signalman 3rd Class.
Lucieer, Lucien Peter. Yeoman 2nd Class.

Main Deck Aft[1]

Barek, Walter Paul. Boatswain's Mate 1st Class.
Underwood, James Edward. Seaman 2nd Class.

Notes

Notes to the Introduction

[1] The formal name of a Higgins boat is LCPV for Landing Craft, Vehicle and Personnel. It was a wooden boat or landing craft with a flat steel bow in the front that dropped to make a ramp. The Higgins boat was 36 feet and 3 inches long, and 10 feet, 10 inches wide, and could carry 36 men or 8 tons of cargo. The Higgins boat is named for its inventor, Andrew Jackson Higgins of New Orleans.

[2] Quoted in Nathan Miller, *War at Sea: A Naval History of World War II* (New York: Scribner, 1995), 425.

Notes to Chapter One

[1] E.B. Potter, *The Naval Academy Illustrated History of the United States Navy* (New York: Galahad Books, 1971), 10.

[2] Ibid., 26-27.

[3] The Navy's General Board existed only from 1909 until 1915. The board was composed of senior naval officers, and advised the civilian Secretary of the Navy on matters of personnel, operations, supplies and equipment, and inspections. The office of Chief of Naval Operations superseded the General Board in 1915.

[4] Norman Friedman, *U.S. Battleships: An Illustrated Design History* (Annapolis, Md.: Naval Institute Press, 1985), 75, 85, 93.

[5] Office of Superintending Constructor for United States Navy, Newport News Shipbuilding and Dry Dock Company, *General Information U.S.S. "Texas"* (Newport News, Virginia, 1914), x. Hereinafter cited as *General Information*.

[6] "Texas, Our Greatest Warship, Launched," *New York Times*, May 19, 1912.

[7] *General Information*, x.

[8] *General Information*, 6; Henderson B. Gregory, "U.S.S. *Texas* Description and Official Trials," *Journal of the American Society of Naval Engineers* 26:1 (1914), 48-53.

[9] U.S.S. *Texas* Log Book, March 1914.

[10] *General Information*, 1-3, 26.

[11] "Booklet of General Plans, 1935, updated 1944," (Puget Sound Naval Shipyard, 1944), copy in the Battleship *Texas* Archives, San Jacinto Battleground State Historic Site, LaPorte, Texas.

[12] Theodore C. Mason, *Battleship Sailor* (Annapolis, Md.: Naval Institute Press, 1982) 3.

[13] *General Information*, 5.

[14] Officers of the United States Navy, *Naval Ordnance: A Textbook Prepared for the Use of the Midshipmen of the United States Naval Academy* (Annapolis, Md.: The United States Naval Institute, 1934), 576-77, 604-606.

[15] Ibid., 576-78.

[16] Ibid., 585-88.

[17] H.C. Ramsey, *Elementary Naval Ordnance and Gunnery* (Boston: Little, Brown, and Company, 1918), 108-10; Officers, *Naval Ordnance*, 331-32.

[18] Officers, *Naval Ordnance*, 325, 332.

[19] Ibid., Chapter XV, Plate I.

[20] *General Information*, 5; Ramsey, *Elementary*, 288-92; Deck Log, U.S.S. *Texas*; Frederick J. Milford, "U.S. Navy Torpedoes, Part One: Torpedoes Through the Thirties," *The Submarine Review* (April 1996), 65.

[21] *General Information*, 5.

[22] A barbette is an armored vertical cylinder upon which rests the gun turret. The barbette protects the hoists that supply gunpowder and projectiles to the guns in the turret.

[23] The conning tower was an enclosed observation and command post on a ship, from which the ship could be controlled. The armored conning tower was theoretically the safest place on the ship.

[24] *General Information*, 3.

[25] Ibid., 5; Gregory, "U.S.S. *Texas*," Table III.

[26] Gregory, "U.S.S. *Texas*," 36.

Notes to Chapter Two

[1] J. Robert Moskin, *The U.S. Marine Corps Story* (New York: McGraw Hill, 1987), 157-59. Ironically, April 21 is the anniversary of the Battle of San Jacinto in 1836. On that date Gen. Sam Houston led an army of Texans who defeated the Mexican Army under Gen. Antonio Lopez de Santa Ana. Houston's victory led to Texas independence from Mexico.

[2] *Dictionary of American Naval Fighting Ships*, Volume VII (Washington: Naval History Center, 1981), 115 (hereinafter cited as *DANFS*); G.H. Vuitch Diary, May 12-23, 1914, Battleship *Texas* Archives, San Jacinto Battleground State Historic Site, La Porte, Texas.

[3] D.T. Mervine, "A Word to Messengers," *Wells Fargo Messenger*, January 1915, p. 85.

[4] *DANFS*, 115; Deck Logs, U.S.S. *Texas*, microfilm copy, Battleship *Texas* Archives. The Deck Log was a hardcover, bound journal kept on the quarterdeck when in port or on the navigation deck when at sea. In it, the officer of the deck kept notes on everything that happened on the ship. Originals reside in the National Archives.

[5] The 12,500-ton *Ryndam* was quickly repaired and put back into transatlantic passenger service, sailing the Amsterdam to New York line. In the spring of 1916 the ship was damaged when it ran into a mine off the coast of England, but was able to continue on to Rotterdam. Then in August 1917 the United States chartered the *Ryndam* to carry troops to the war in France. See "The First World War," The Unofficial Homepage, Holland-America Line, available on-line at: www.unofficial.net/hal/line4.html accessed August 22, 2001.

[6] Department of Commerce, Bureau of Navigation, Radio Service, *Important Events in Radiotelegraphy* (Washington: Government Printing Office, 1916); Vuitch Diary, May 25, 1915; Warren Hughes, "A 'Medal' for U.S.S. *Texas*," *Houston Chronicle*, September 5, 1948.

[7] Deck Log, July 31, 1916. Insert description of boat-crane derrick posts.

[8] Jerry Jones, *U.S. Battleship Operations in World War I* (Annapolis, Md.: Naval Institute Press, 1998), 3-16.

[9] *DANFS*, 114; Paul Schubert, *Come on, Texas,* 2nd ed. (Kingsport, Tenn.: Kingsport Press, 1942), 97-99; Admiral Bernard H. Bieri, oral history, U.S. Naval History Institute.

[10] *DANFS*, 114.

[11] Jones, *U.S. Battleship Operations*, 113.

[12] Norman Freidman, *U.S. Battleships: An Illustrated Design History* (Annapolis, Md.: Naval Institute Press, 1985), 176.

[13] *A Brief History of the U.S.S.* Texas: *and Life Generally in the North Sea During a War* (n.p., [1919]), 24-28.

[14] Ibid., 28-34.

[15] Ibid., 36-40.

[16] *DANFS*, 114; *Brief History,* 44-50.

[17] *Brief History,* 51-53.

[18] *DANFS*, 114; *Brief History*, 57-58.

[19] *Brief History*, 65-68.

[20] Ibid., 72, 74.

[21] Ibid., 88-92; *DANFS*, 114.

[22] *DANFS*, 114-15; Jones, *U.S. Battleship Operations*, 38; *Brief History*, 104-107.

Notes to Chapter Three

[1] Gerald E. Wheeler, *Admiral William Veazie Pratt, U.S. Navy: A Sailor's Life* (Washington, D.C.: Naval History Division, Department of the Navy, 1974), 137.

[2] *A Brief History of the U.S.S.* Texas: *and Life Generally in the North Sea During a War* (n.p., [1919]), 53.

[3] Ibid., 80-81.

[4] *Dictionary of American Naval Fighting Ships*, Volume VII (Washington: Naval History Center, 1981), 115. Hereinafter cited as *DANFS*; Andrew Krepinevich, "Transforming to Victory: The U.S. Navy, Carrier Aviation, and Preparing for War in the Pacific," (Cambridge, Mass.: The Olin Institute, 2000), available on-line at: www.csbaonline.org/4Publications/Archive/A.20000000.Transforming_to_Vi/A.20000000.Transforming_to_Vi.htm

[5] *DANFS*, 115.

[6] Manley R. Irwin, "The Naval Policies of the Harding Administration: Time For a Reassessment?" *International Journal of Naval History* 1:1 (April 2002), available on-line at: www.ijnhonline.org/volume1_number1_Apr02/article_irwin_harding_policies.doc.htm

[7] Conference on the Limitation of Armament, Washington, November 12, 1921-February 6, 1922 [Washington Naval Treaty], full text available on-line at: www.ibiblio.org/pha/pre-war/1922/nav_lim.html

[8] Wheeler, *Admiral William Veazie Pratt*, 204.

[9] Ibid., 171-72, 218; *DANFS*, 116

[10] Norman Friedman, *U.S. Battleships: An Illustrated Design History* (Annapolis, Md.: Naval Institute Press, 1985), 420.

[11] Ibid., 189.

[12] Washington Naval Treaty.

[13] Henry A. Wiley, *An Admiral From Texas* (Garden City, N.Y.: Doubleday, Doran and Company, 1934) 1, 4, 10, 24, 275-76.

[14] Ibid., 277-80.

[15] Ibid., 280-81.

[16] Ibid., 281-84.

[17] Ibid., 284-85.

[18] Ibid., 302.

[19] Wheeler, *Admiral William Veazie Pratt*, 283.

[20] Ibid., 289-92.

[21] Ibid., 292.

[22] Samuel Eliot Morison, *History of United States Naval Operations in World War II, Volume III: The Rising Sun in the Pacific* (Boston: Little Brown and Company, 1948), 60, 140.

[23] Wheeler, *Admiral William Veazie Pratt*, 2, 7, 293.

[24] Ibid., 296-301.

[25] *DANFS*, 116.

[26] Ibid.

Notes to Chapter Four

[1] Brigadier Peter Young, ed., *The World Almanac Book of World War II* (Englewood Cliffs, N.J.; Prentice-Hall, 1981), 12-15.

[2] F.R. Smith, "A Most Embarrassing Situation," *The Paint Chipper* 8:3 (2001), 8.

[3] Deck Log, U.S.S. *Texas*, microfilm copy, Battleship *Texas* Archives, San Jacinto Battleground State Historic Site, LaPorte, Texas.

Notes to Chapter Five

[1] U.S.S. *Texas* Log Book, Battleship *Texas* Archives, San Jacinto Battleground State Historic Site, LaPorte, Texas (hereinafter cited as "Log Book").

[2] Russell A. Morehouse to Battleship *Texas*, letter, n.d., Battleship *Texas* Archives.

[3] Log Book.

[4] Tom Koltuniak, interview by author, February 1, 2000, Battleship *Texas* Archives.

[5] *The United States Ship Texas in World War II* (Welfare Fund, U.S.S. *Texas*, 1946). Hereinafter cited as *Cruise Book*; Walter H. Zessin, Battleship *Texas* Questionnaire, 1988, Battleship *Texas* Archives; Morehouse letter.

[6] "U.S.S. *Texas* Special Bulletin," *U.S.S. Texas Morning Press*, December 27, 1941.

[7] Deck Logs, U.S.S. *Texas*, microfilm copy, Battleship *Texas* Archives; Secret War Diary, U.S.S. *Texas*, microfilm copy, Battleship *Texas* Archives. The Secret War Diary was the classified version of the Deck Log. Original copies reside in the National Archives.

[8] Deck Log.

[9] Deck Log.

[10] Daily War Diary, U.S.S. *Texas*, microfilm copy, Battleship *Texas* Archives. After December 7, 1941, the Navy Department changed the name of "Deck Logs" to "Daily War Diary." Hereinafter cited as "Daily War Diary."

[11] Daily War Diary.

[12] Daily War Diary.

Notes to Chapter Six

[1] Leo J. Meyer, "The Decision To Invade North Africa (TORCH)," *Command Decisions*, ed. Kent Robert Greenfield (Washington D.C: Center of Military History, United States Army, 1960), 174.

[2] Ibid.

[3] Ibid., 175.

[4] Ibid.

[5] Ibid., 181.

[6] Ibid., 183.

[7] Ibid., 186-87.

[8] Samuel Eliot Morison, *Operations in North African Waters, October 1942-June 1943*, vol. 2 of *History of United States Naval Operations in World War II* (Boston: Little, Brown and Company, 1948), 12-14.

[9] Dwight D. Eisenhower, *Crusade in Europe* (Garden City, N.Y.: Doubleday & Company, 1949), 80-82.

[10] Ibid., 82-83; Morison, *Operations*, 17.

[11] George F. Howe, *United States Army in World War II: The Mediterranean Theater of Operations—Northwest Africa: Seizing The Initiative in the West* (Washington, D.C.: Center of Military History, United States Army, 1957), 40-41.

[12] Daily War Diary, U.S.S. *Texas*, September 28-October 3, 1942, October 14, 1942, October 17, 1942, microfilm copy, Battleship *Texas* Archives, San Jacinto Battleground State Historic Site, LaPorte, Texas.

[13] Ibid., October 23, 1942.

[14] Ibid., October 24, 1942.

[15] Ibid., October 26-27, 1942.

[16] Ibid., October 30-November 5, 1942.

[17] Morison, *Operations*, 50-51, 118-19.

[18] "Resume of the Happenings in the North African Theatre Since 0100 Sunday, November 8, 1942," *U.S.S. Texas Morning Press,* November 15, 1942, p. 3.

[19] Morison, *Operations*, 117-18.

[20] Ibid., 121-23.

[21] Capt. Roy Pfaff, commanding officer U.S.S. *Texas*, to Commander Northern Attack Group, "Battle Report of Action at Mehdia, French Morocco, 7 to 11 November 1942 Inclusive," report dated November 19, 1942, p. 2, Battleship *Texas* Archives.

[22] Ibid.

[23] Ibid., 2-6; Morison, *Operations*, 126.

[24] Pfaff, "Battle Report," 3.

[25] Ibid., 3; Morison, *Operations*, 132.

[26] Pfaff, "Battle Report," 4; Ens. L.D. Hollingsworth, Jr., "U.S. Aircraft-Action With Enemy," report dated November 10, 1942, Battleship *Texas* Archives.

[27] Pfaff, "Battle Report," 4; Lt. W.R. Turner, "U.S. Aircraft-Action With Enemy," report dated November 10, 1942, Battleship *Texas* Archives.

[28] Pfaff, "Battle Report," 4; L.R. Chesley, Jr., "U.S. Aircraft-Action With Enemy," report dated November 10, 1942, Battleship *Texas* Archives.

[29] Mark Emery Been, Battleship *Texas* Questionnaire, 1988, Battleship *Texas* Archives; Mark Been, interview by author, October 7, 2000, transcript, Battleship *Texas* Archives; Daily War Diary, November 12, 1942.

[30] Eisenhower, *Crusade in Europe*, 104, 107.

[31] Will John Eddleman, interview by author, March 1, 2001, transcript, Battleship *Texas* Archives.

[32] Morison, *Operations,* 133; James Zampell, "Invasion at Porty Lyautey, Morocco-Prize and Salvage Attempt," *The Paint Chipper,* September 6, 1999, p. 5.

[33] Zampell, "Invasion," 5; Daily War Diary, November 19, 1942.

Notes to Chapter Seven

[1] Daily War Diary, January 1944, microfilm copy, Battleship *Texas* Archives, San Jacinto Battleground State Historic Site, LaPorte, Texas.

[2] Ibid., January-March 1944.

[3] Ibid., March-April 1944.

[4] Ibid., April 1944.

[5] Ibid.

[6] Lt. Commander W. Denton, Jr., "VO-VS Pilots as Ship-to-Shore Bombardment Spotters," report dated July 28, 1944, Battleship *Texas* Archives.

[7] Daily War Diary, May 1944.

[8] David C.S. Kline, Battleship *Texas* Questionnaire, 1988, Battleship *Texas* Archives.

[9] Gen. Dwight D. Eisenhower, address to the crew of the U.S.S. *Texas*, Belfast Lough, Northern Ireland, June 1944, copy in Battleship *Texas* Archives.

[10] *The United States Ship Texas in World War II* (Welfare Fund, U.S.S. *Texas*, 1946). Hereinafter cited as "Cruise Book."

[11] Daily War Diary, May 1944.

[12] "Address Made By the Captain to the Crew of the Texas," May 31, 1944, copy in Battleship *Texas* Archives.

[13] "U.S.S. *Texas* Action Report for Period 3-17 June, 1944," copy in Battleship *Texas* Archives; Daily War Diary, June 1944; Chaplain LeGrande Moody, unpublished manuscript, 13-16, Battleship *Texas* Archives; Glenn Longendelpher Diary, Battleship *Texas* Archives; Emery Nester, unpublished manuscript, 17-21, Battleship *Texas* Archives.

[14] Will John Eddleman, interview by author, March 1, 2001, Houston, tape recording, Battleship *Texas* Archives.

[15] Richard B. Derickson, Battleship *Texas* Questionnaire, 1988, Battleship *Texas* Archives.

[16] "U.S.S. *Texas* Action Report for Period 3-17 June 1944," Battleship *Texas* Archives.

[17] Ronald J. Drez, ed., *Voices of D-Day: The Story of the Allied Invasion Told by Those Who Were There* (Baton Rouge: Louisiana State University Press, 1994), 200.

[18] "U.S.S. *Texas* Action Report for Period 3-17 June, 1944."

[19] A.B. Feuer, "The Valiant *Texas*: Battleship Guns at Normandy," *Military Heritage* (August 1999), 80-82.

[20] James A. Naismith, interview by Tim Holland, October 8, 2000, transcript, Battleship *Texas* Archives.

[21] "U.S.S. *Texas* Action Report for Period 3-17 June, 1944."

[22] Moody manuscript, 18-20.

[23] "U.S.S. *Texas* Action Report for Period 3-17 June, 1944"; Moody manuscript; Daily War Diary.

[24] Roy Robbins Diary, Battleship *Texas* Archives.

[25] Daily War Diary; Moody manuscript, 22-23.

[26] "U.S.S. *Texas* Action Report for Period June 3-17, 1944"; Naismith interview; Clarence E. Bachman, Jr., interview by author, December 6, 1999, transcript, Battleship *Texas* Archives.

[27] Naismith interview; Daily War Diary.

[28] Omar N. Bradley and Clay Blair, *A General's Life* (New York: Simon and Schuster, 1983), 249.

[29] Bachman interview.

[30] Naismith interview.

[31] Daily War Diary.

[32] Ibid.

[33] Bradley and Blair, *General's Life*, 251.

Notes to Chapter Eight

[1] Daily War Diary, microfilm copy, Battleship *Texas* Archives, San Jacinto Battleground State Historic Site, LaPorte, Texas; Emery Nester, unpublished manuscript, 45, Battleship *Texas* Archives.

[2] "U.S.S. *Texas* Action Report off Cherbourg, France, 25 June 1944," copy in the Battleship *Texas* Archives. Hereinafter cited as "Cherbourg Action Report."

[3] Ibid.

[4] Daily War Diary; "Cherbourg Action Report."

[5] Chaplain LeGrande Moody, transcript of taped reminiscence, *Battleship* Texas Archives.

[6] Moody transcript.

[7] Daily War Diary; "Cherbourg Action Report."

[8] Moody transcript.

[9] Will John Eddleman, interview by author, March 1, 2001, Houston, tape recording, Battleship *Texas* Archives.

[10] Ibid.; Martin Sommers, "Hard Right Rudder!...All Hands Below!" *Saturday Evening Post*, September 16, 1944, 109.

[11] Moody transcript.

[12] "Cherbourg Action Report."

[13] Sgt. Maj. Viekko Liila, interview by author, October 24, 2000, transcript, Battleship *Texas* Archives.

[14] Stephen A. Sturdevant, letter to the author, March 28, 2001, original in Battleship *Texas* Archives.

[15] Roy Robbins Diary, Battleship *Texas* Archives; Glenn Longendelpher Diary, Battleship *Texas* Archives.

[16] Daily War Diary.

[17] Robbins Diary.

[18] Jeffrey J. Clarke, *Southern France: 15 August-14 September 1944* (Washington: U.S. Army Center of Military History), 2-4.

[19] Ibid.

[20] "U.S.S. *Texas* Action Report, Southern Coast of France, from 1500 on 11 August 1944, to Midnight 16 August 1944," Battleship *Texas* Archives. Hereinafter cited as "Southern France Action Report."

[21] Ibid.; Robbins Diary.

[22] "Southern France Action Report."

[23] Robbins Diary.

[24] Daily War Diary.

[25] "Routine for Thursday, September 7, 1944," copy in Battleship *Texas* Archives.

Notes to Chapter Nine

[1] Daily War Diary, microfilm copy, Battleship *Texas* Archives, San Jacinto Battleground State Historic Site, LaPorte, Texas.

[2] Ibid.

[3] Ralph Fletcher, interview by author, August 2, 2000, transcript, Battleship *Texas* Archives.

[4] Roy E. Appleman, *Okinawa: The Last Battle* (Washington, D.C.: The Center of Military History, United States Army, 1948), 3-4.

[5] Daily War Diary.

[6] "U.S.S. *Texas* Action Report Covering the Invasion of the Island of Iwo Jima for the Period of 10 February 1945 to 10 March 1945," copy in the Battleship *Texas* Archives. Hereinafter cited as "Iwo Jima Action Report."

[7] Harold C. Long, interview by Tim Holland, October 7, 2000, transcript, Battleship *Texas* Archives.

[8] "Iwo Jima Action Report."

[9] Ibid.

[10] Ibid; Whitman S. Bartley, *Iwo Jima: Amphibious Epic* (Quantico, Va.: Historical Branch, U.S.Marine Corps, 1954), 51.

[11] E.A. McCampbell, interview by author, transcript, Battleship *Texas* Archives.

[12] Eneva Limerick, interview by author, transcript, Battleship *Texas* Archives.

[13] Fletcher interview.

[14] Bartley, *Iwo Jima*, 54-55.

[15] Tom Koltuniak, interview by author, February 1, 2000, transcript, Battleship *Texas* Archives.

[16] Ibid.

[17] "Iwo Jima Action Report."

[18] James A. Naismith, interview by Tim Holland, October 8, 2000, transcript, Battleship *Texas* Archives.

[19] Ralph Fletcher, interview by author, October 2000, transcript, Battleship *Texas* Archives.

[20] Ed Reichert, interview by author, Houston, October 7, 2000, transcript, Battleship *Texas* Archives.

[21] Bartley, *Iwo Jima*, 113, 210.

Notes to Chapter Ten

[1] James A. Naismith, interview by Tim Holland, October 8, 2000, transcript, Battleship *Texas* Archives, San Jacinto Battleground State Historic Site, LaPorte, Texas.

[2] Capt. Charles Baker, "U.S.S. *Texas* Action Report, Landing on and Subsequent Capture of Okinawa, 21 March 1945 to 14 May 1945," copy in the Battleship *Texas* Archives. Hereinafter cited as "Okinawa Action Report."

[3] Ibid.

[4] Ralph Fletcher, interview by author, August 2, 2000, transcript, Battleship *Texas* Archives; Naismith interview.

[5] Charles S. Nichols, Jr., *Okinawa: Victory in the Pacific* (Quantico, Va.: Historical Branch, U.S. Marine Corps, 1955), 63, 64; "Okinawa Action Report."

[6] Robert Leckie, *Okinawa: The Last Battle of World War II* (New York: Viking, 1995), 69.

[7] Ibid., 70.

[8] Eneva Limerick, interview by author, transcript, Battleship *Texas* Archives.

[9] John Monsies, interview by author, transcript, Battleship *Texas* Archives.

[10] "Okinawa Action Report."

[11] Ibid.

[12] Fletcher interview.

[13] "Okinawa Action Report"; Naismith interview.

[14] Tom Koltuniak, interview by author, February 1, 2000, transcript, Battleship *Texas* Archives.

[15] Daily War Diary, microfilm copy, Battleship *Texas* Archives; "Okinawa Action Report."

[16] Fletcher interview.

[17] "Okinawa Action Report."

[18] Ibid.; Daily War Diary.

[19] "Okinawa Action Report."

[20] Ibid.

[21] Endorsement to CO Report, From Commander Battleship Division Five to Commander in Chief, United States Fleet, May 26, 1945, copy in the Battleship *Texas* Archives.

Notes to Chapter Eleven

[1] W.C. Black, interview by author, transcript, Battleship *Texas* Archives, San Jacinto Battleground State Historic Site, LaPorte, Texas; Al Alexander, interview by author, transcript, Battleship *Texas* Archives.

[2] Eneva Limerick, interview by author, transcript, Battleship *Texas* Archives; Will John Eddleman, interview by author, March 1, 2001, Houston, tape recording, Battleship *Texas* Archives.

[3] James A. Naismith, interview by Tim Holland, October 8, 2000, transcript, Battleship *Texas* Archives.

[4] Daily War Diary, microfilm copy, Battleship *Texas* Archives.

[5] Ibid.

[6] Naismith interview.

Notes to Chapter Twelve

[1] Texas Legislature, House Bill Number 623, 1947.

[2] "Battleship Texas Becomes State Shrine," *The Houston Chronicle*, April 21, 1948.

[3] Harold Scarlett, "The *Texas* Needs Major Overhaul, Official Says," *Houston Post*, December 8, 1984.

[4] Ed Morrison, letter to author, May 29, 2005, Battleship *Texas* Archives, San Jacinto Battleground State Historic Site, LaPorte, Texas.

[5] Ibid.

Notes to Appendix B

[1] Suffered blast concussion from firing of ship's guns while fighting fire on the main deck.

Index

CPSIA information can be obtained
at www.ICGtesting.com
Printed in the USA
LVOW12s1615031117
554901LV00002B/320/P